101 WAYS TO
NEGOTIATE MORE
EFFECTIVELY

This book is dedicated to my late father, who taught me my first steps in negotiation. He taught me the work ethic and showed me by example how to love hard work.

101 WAYS TO
NEGOTIATE MORE
EFFECTIVELY

DAVID OLIVER

KOGAN
PAGE

YOURS TO HAVE AND TO HOLD

BUT NOT TO COPY

Although masculine pronouns are used throughout this book for ease of expression, feminine pronouns are equally applicable.

First published in 1996
Reprinted in 1997

Kogan Page Limited
120 Pentonville Road
London N1 9JN

British Library Cataloguing in Publication Data

A CIP record for this book is available from the British Library.

ISBN 0 7494 2100 2

Typeset by Saxon Graphics Ltd, Derby
Printed in England by Clays Ltd, St Ives plc

Contents

Introduction

If you are reading this book the chances are that you are in business. Everyone in business invariably both buys and sells. Most business owners, managers, partners buy and sell in different ways every week, sometimes every day. This book is for you, to help you get the best out of every deal whether it is a one-off deal, or a long-term relationship. It is also for the professional salesman or buyer.

Each of the 101 Ways has been written specifically so that it has application for selling and buying. Apply the principles in this book and you should quite easily see an improvement in your net profit of at least 10 per cent. No, I am not exaggerating, so please do not switch off! Just one idea alone has saved me £50,000 on the cost of biscuits! (See Way 49.)

Very few business people negotiate effectively, and the rewards are great for those who do. Follow these principles and above average performance will follow. A 10 per cent improvement is well within your grasp, so read on!

One trend today in modern business practice is based around partnerships between suppliers and customers. To enjoy a long-term relationship, both buyer and seller must reach mutual agreement about the business being transacted — not just price but a whole range of terms, conditions and other related ingredients. To do that they negotiate. The skill of the negotiators will determine whether that relationship succeeds or fails. The greater your skill, the greater the advantage you can expect.

Many of you reading this book will have ideas or examples of your own. I would love to hear from you. Why not write to me at Kogan Page — maybe I can use your anecdote in the first revision!

Definition

Way 1 Know what negotiation is

There are many misconceptions about negotiation. Estate agents like to call themselves 'negotiators', yet in house sales they rarely do anything, except discount the price of the property. Many salesmen describe themselves as negotiators. So what is it? Is it a Dutch auction which starts high and goes lower? Is it another word for selling? These are very common misconceptions. In fact negotiation is none of these. A simple dictionary definition describes negotiation as 'discussing or bargaining in order to reach agreement'.

Negotiation is a transaction in which both parties have a veto on the final outcome. It requires voluntary consent on both sides. It is a give and take process where the actual conditions of a transaction are agreed. It is the act or process of bargaining to reach a mutually acceptable agreement or objective. It requires movement on both sides — real or perceived.

Why do we negotiate? Simply because if we don't we will not get the best deals available to us. One thing I can promise you is, *if you don't negotiate, you are already losing money.* In a free market economy there are only two pivots around which any deal will finally be agreed: price and value. The bulk of people in business concentrate just on price — wrongly.

Negotiation is in some ways like chess. You are prepared to sacrifice particular pieces in the interests of winning the game. In chess you know the pieces but you can't see into the other person's mind. In negotiation you don't necessarily know the 'pieces'. You have to discover and develop your own pieces and find ways of uncovering your counterpart's.

Way 2 Know what it isn't

Negotiation is not selling. Negotiation begins when the sale has been adequately made. Selling skills are different and are covered in *101 Ways to Increase Your Sales* in this series.

The simple test is the way buyer and seller relate to each other. In the selling phase, one person is persuading, the other is being persuaded. In true negotiation, the attitude of both is the same — both want to reach agreement. The question is not whether to buy or not. The question becomes, 'On what terms can I buy or sell?'

Negotiation assumes that there is already an established desire to buy and an ability to supply. The whole emphasis moves towards profit implications and specific terms or arrangements.

Sales people frequently fail to realise when the role of seller changes to that of negotiator, and it costs them. I asked scores of people for anecdotes on negotiation. Most of the salespeople struggled to find one. Many of them said, 'I do it intuitively'. When I questioned them in detail, the truth was they did not recognise this transition from selling to negotiation. As a result in every case they were not effective.

Negotiation is not 'giving in' or conceding. Concession can imply surrender on another person's terms. If we view negotiation as surrendering it will condition our thinking, our approach will be weak and our deals will not be effective. That does not mean we won't move in our negotiation — we will. But our movement must never be giving in or moving 'one way'.

Negotiation is not about digging our heels in. If we are inflexible we will be met by equal inflexibility. Showing our strength, and wanting to appear tough are not the same as good negotiation. They can reflect our own insecurity and will either lead to immediate deadlock, or they will be exploited by our counterpart, and rightly so. Negotiation doesn't just relate to agreeing terms in the buying process; it can also relate to disputed ownership or late/non-payment.

Way 3 Win Win

Two possibilities exist about the way we view the negotiation process. The moderately aggressive stance is where we look out primarily for a strong gain for ourselves. The Win Win concept is where we look for our best interest, but in which we understand that the other person's interests, if served well, can often serve ours even better. To be effective, both parties must feel they have won.

I was introduced to this personally, when one of my clients asked me to launch a company. He never offered me a salary, he asked me to write my own proposal taking into account the fact that he wanted me to be as motivated as possible to get the best possible return for him as investor. Not only did it force certain issues in my own thinking, it put a strong sense of responsibility on my shoulders. My client looked at the proposal I made, and found one or two ways where he believed he could improve my motivation — he was right.

Good negotiation is not about getting everything your own way. It is about balancing each other. You don't defer to your counterpart and allow him to get all that he wants, you have your own aspirations which you must secure. That requires two way movement which produces Win Win. It affects the business relationship positively. It also enables us to achieve not just more sales, or better supply but more importantly, the growth in profit that we are all looking for.

In effective negotiation we should not only be concerned about our own goals and objectives. We should have a genuine interest in, and a good grasp of what the other party is hoping for or aiming for. The more we can help the other person to achieve what he wants, the more likely we are to achieve what we are looking for from the deal. Some trainers assert that you should focus on your own position only. The logic behind this is that the other person is the only one who knows what is best for him. That is probably true with skilled negotiators, but with inexperienced negotiators genuine two-way concern is often necessary.

The more genuine interest we can show in the other person and his aspirations, the less threatened he will be, the more he will volunteer information and the more likely we are to reach an ideal solution. If you can think Win Win rather than Win-Lose you will become more effective, less stressed and always better in the long term.

This was graphically illustrated by a software developer who worked for his client for two or three years. It seemed that at every opportunity, the client would try to screw more discount, more value, more price reductions. The software developer got fed up with the approach and allowed his feelings to dictate his approach. He dug his heels in, and focused on his own interests. The result was alienation. Had there been frank dialogue, if both parties could have thought through what was important to the other, an amicable and profitable solution would have easily been found.

Count the Cost

Great gain is to be had from negotiating, but only if the task is done effectively. There is a cost in terms of resolve, priorities, time, preparation, forward planning. At the heart of effective negotiation, there has to be a calculation of what is involved and the price that has to be paid, usually before the negotiation begins.

When I train I use the word 'COST' as an acronym. It acts as a useful memory jog reminding us of the four ingredients that represent the practical outworking of the cost involved: Commitment, Objective, Strategy, Tactics.

Way 4 Commitment

Commitment to the negotiation process is essential. This applies to negotiation as an overall process. It also applies specifically to a particular negotiation in hand. A half-hearted approach can never be effective. There must be a serious commitment to achieving the result you want. If you are serious then you will be taken seriously, if you are casual then you will be taken casually.

In my experience, most business people do not have true commitment to the negotiation process. What typically happens is that negotiation gets the odd few moments, the remnants of our time. To be effective we need to settle the issue that negotiation is going to require predetermined amounts of time and resource.

Overall commitment
We must determine what our overall business goals are, and what levels of profit, volume, price, saving or improvement we are aiming for. This requires thinking through the key areas.

Commitment to a particular negotiation in hand
I was eating at an Indian restaurant recently as part of a group which someone else had responsibility for. During the process of ordering, one person said, 'Let's ask for a special deal before we order and try to get a good selection for £10 each'. The leader of the party was unsure. Essentially, he was uncomfortable with the suggestion, so a vague proposal was made something like, ' We would like 10 per cent discount please'. There was no commitment in the request and the waiter said nothing. Nothing was agreed.

The approach was treated casually because that is exactly what it was. When the bill was presented at the end, there was no discount. When pressed, the waiter simply said that the manager was away and he had no authority to give discount. The meal cost nearly £20 per head. It cost us all because there was no commitment to the negotiation. It was treated hopefully, casually, and therefore without authority.

Way 5 Objective

Once the issue of commitment is settled we must have clear objectives. Otherwise we will invariably settle for less than we need to. Not being sure of what we want is a common reason for getting poor negotiated results. Ask for more and you get more, ask for less and you get less. If you don't have clear objectives you won't know where to aim, and in every negotiation you will end up 'shooting from the hip'. This will always reduce your authority and will also leave you feeling less than confident. You will get less.

Objectives for your company
We need to establish clearly what our company objectives are, what business it is in. This can cover many areas but in the context of negotiation we need to have an overall objective, which states our profit levels, the type of business or supply that we want. The type of product or service. The levels at which we want to buy and sell.

One legitimate objective would be for a business manager, an owner, or a buyer to aim to reduce overall costs by 15 per cent while improving specific elements of supply. On the other hand, an owner or salesman could have an objective of increasing the value of every sale by 10 per cent. By that I don't mean more sales, I mean better sales. More sales is also a good objective but it is not primarily a negotiation related objective. The two could comfortably sit together.

Objectives for the negotiation in hand
Before we start negotiation we must know what our goals or objectives are. What is our ideal position, how can we support it or defend it? What are the objectives on price, on delivery, on volume, on frequency? What do we want to achieve from the other person? The clearer these objectives are, the more likely you are to ask for them and the more likely it is that you will get them. The more you ask for what you want the more you will get.

Way 6 Strategy

Strategy for the company
Once we have clear objectives for our company we must then put a strategy in place. Our strategy is simply a series of preplanned steps which enable us to realise those objectives. In other words, we know exactly what to do, when to do it and how, in order to achieve what we have set ourselves. In broad terms it will include:

- Defining which person or people are responsible for the negotiation process
- Training the person or people responsible for the negotiation process
- Planning for negotiation with existing long-term business relationships
- Putting times in the diary for review meetings with customers/suppliers.

My good friend Nick Robinson, Chairman of the Marketing Guild, talks about the five-month itch and the nine-month itch in any long-term relationship. What he is referring to is the fact that there is bound to be dissatisfaction in any long-term relationship at particular points. The five-month itch occurs for a variety of reasons. Maybe the supplier has not quite met his deadlines. Maybe the buyer's aspirations have not been matched.

The supplier in this case should be defending his corner. He should stay in contact regularly. He should provide reams of paper showing results, reports, savings, improvements. He should also stay close, visiting in person every two or three weeks. Around the nine-month point in any contractual relationship, the supplier should be aware that a good buyer is already considering other companies, prices are coming in and preliminary negotiations may well be taking place. Now is the time to romance your client like mad.

If you are the buyer in the relationship, you should be gathering information that will help in a review process, information that will help in the inevitable impending new negotiation phase.

Whether you are the buyer or supplier there is an opportunity here for you. Why not build in a quarterly review, which you drive? You set the agenda, you control the process. Call it a 'health check' and increase your negotiation power in the process.

Strategy for the particular negotiation in hand
Our objective for this particular negotiation must be crystal clear and we must know exactly how we intend to achieve it:

- Who will conduct the negotiation for us?

- What information do we need about the other party and how will we secure it?

- What experts or specialists do we want to take?

- How do we ensure that we are controlling the whole process?

- Where should we hold the meeting?

- What do we need in print?

- What is our bottom line?

- What is our ideal Win/Win outcome?

Way 7 Tactics

Every negotiation has a tactical element. Every situation is different and how we read it will condition our success. Many tactics are provided in this book. Think through which ones are likely to be most effective. We need to know which tactics we want to use, which ones are favoured by us and which ones our opposite number is likely to be using. Before a particular negotiation, skim through these tactics. Jot down the ones that seem most appropriate, think through how you might use them, or how they might be used against you.

Late one Friday night I spoke to a client who had a meeting with a potential buyer for his company on Monday. He wanted some guidelines, so we chatted through all the possible tactics he could use and which ones his counterpart might use. Within ten minutes or so he was confident that he had the right approach. Those ten minutes will have dramatically affected his performance on the Monday — time well spent.

Six Key Elements

Way 8 Prepare

If you negotiate casually you will never optimise your effectiveness. The more important the negotiation, the more preparation you should do. If you have not prepared properly and the other person has, you are at a disadvantage immediately. It will make you feel unprofessional and weak, and to be honest, at that moment you are. Lack of preparation will nearly always cost you money.

When we prepare, we need to ask ourselves questions about the other person. We must form a judgement about what may or may not be important to that person:

- What is important to them in making their decision?

- Where will they seek to negotiate?

- What combination of factors is likely to be important: cost, price, quantities, delivery, exclusive terms, credit, stockholding, training, confidentiality, after sales, maintenance, guarantees, contract length.

- Seek to uncover preferences, needs, obstacles, opportunities and problems. In each of these five cases ask how they could be related to the negotiation in hand.

We also need to prepare our own position. What is our objective? What price level are we aiming for? Good negotiators have an ideal objective, which still enables a Win Win outcome. They have also thought through a worst case scenario, which is their bottom line, below which they will not go.

We must evaluate where we can shift in the process. We must ensure that we know the cost of everything and anything that we could use in the negotiation. For example, costs of giving on price, cost of changed payment, costs of rear-ranging delivery, in short the cost of every proposed change you could make, or offer that you could give.

Having evaluated the information, effective negotiators plan their approach to trading and concessions. The effective negotiator will hunt out common ground and evaluate long term needs, and as a result will have far more trading options.

Summary
Effective negotiation will depend on your accurately identifying at the preparation stage:

- The other person's possible opening statement or position
- How you will move from his opening towards your aspirations
- Your counterpart's potential problems, obstacles, opportunities, needs and preferences
- Your ideal and your bottom line
- The cost of any possible movement you might make and its benefit to your counterpart
- The concessions your counterpart could make and how you might make them appear trivial or worthless.

Way 9 Rehearse

Every major negotiation I have undertaken I have always rehearsed. It is a key to confidence. It is a key to uncovering likely and less likely potential problems and difficulties.

How do you rehearse? Write down your approach. Write down your key statements. Write down your response. What I do is to sit in my office and practise out loud. I will prepare visual material — OHP slides or a simple flip-chart presentation. I will have every key point substantiated or affirmed with facts, figures, pie charts and statistics. I look at all that material with sceptical eyes to see how my approach could be countered or sunk! I make changes.

Try it! Tell yourself what you are going to say, how you will say it, where and in what order. Rehearse how your opposite number might do the same. Try to imagine all the possible responses and develop your counter moves.

An average negotiator will spend approximately the same time as a good one in the preparation phase. An effective negotiator, however, not only gets the information but spends quality time rehearsing various applications of those facts until he is sure that he has the right approach.

I was working for a European client putting together a negotiation in London. We spent hours preparing over the phone and by fax. We produced 35mm OHP slides and print-ed proposal documents. We checked every one and talked through potential weak spots. We were thoroughly pre-pared, but he was still willing to come to London hours early. We sat in the Grosvenor Hotel in Park Lane and rehearsed our individual roles again and again until we were both sure that we had it right. The outcome was superb, but it was no accident. It was down to hours of planned preparation, fol-lowed by hours of planned rehearsal.

Way 10 Describe your position

At some point, each side describes their position clearly. However, your goal should be to let your counterpart talk. Your job is to be in control. You can help yourself by having a written agenda which follows these key elements and puts you automatically in the driving seat. The simplest way to stay in control is to begin by asking questions. The buying and selling has already been done and you normally begin by asking the other person, 'Can we proceed with this as it stands?' In nearly every case the answer is a qualified, 'No'. By the way, if he says, 'Yes' immediately, it probably means you have undershot quite significantly in what you could have achieved.

But he says 'No'. You must then draw him out, get him to describe his position. The more you can get him to talk the better. Try to keep quiet. Don't come back quickly with your own responses. Use positive phrases that will encourage him to keep talking. You might use phrases like, 'I see' or 'Sure, I understand' and then follow it each time with a phrase like,

'What else is important to you in this discussion?' followed by, 'Does that cover all the issues from your point of view?'

Way 11 Propose

If he signals at this stage, you can respond. If he has no proposal of his own, it is your time to make a proposal.

It does not hurt to allow the other person to propose his solution first. It will often cause him to give away concessions too early. It will give us a mirror into his mind, it will give us glimpses of what he is thinking. It will nearly always show up small cracks in his authority or power through which we can later drive the wedge of careful questions.

If the other person presents his position first you have two choices. You can either accept his position and settle for less than you should. Or you can do what you must do and that is to offer your counter proposal.

In many cases his proposal and your response will not be enough to reach agreement. The likelihood is that there will still be a considerable distance between what he wants and what you have counter-proposed. The next few words will make or break you, and those words have to be words that bargain.

Way 12 Bargain

How do we bridge this very real gap, and move both of our interests towards a positive solution? Unskilled negotiators simply give, and the first place they give is price. It's the easy way out, it removes pressure for the moment but it will always cost you.

The only effective response here is for us to *trade* or *bargain*. The dictionary puts it this way 'To *bargain* means to make it a condition of an agreement that something should be done'. If he wants us to move or concede on some of the terms and conditions, then bargaining by its very nature implies that we must get him to move on some of his terms and conditions. I cannot stress this enough because every true negotiation goes through this bargaining phase. This is where your preparation pays off. You have thought through beforehand what you are willing to trade and you have thought through beforehand what you will ask him to trade. Every other approach is conceding not negotiating. This is the pivotal point, this is where you become effective or mediocre. Get this bargaining phase right and you will secure advantage after advantage on every deal you make. Every other approach will without doubt cost you money.

Way 13 Agree

It seems so obvious but so many unskilled negotiators forget to confirm what is agreed. In the intensity of the bargaining process it is easy to forget what has actually been agreed. The objective of every negotiation is to reach agreement. Remember, agreement does not just refer to the final conclusive signing of the deal. There are many points of agreement along the way. Both are important. At every point wherever and whenever you can agree it is important to make the positive point of confirming that agreement.

Make a virtue of every point agreed. Take a bit of time and write it down. Let him know that is what you are doing and let him see you do it. Read it back to confirm it, and sound pleased. For both parties, *en route* agreement is a positive feeling, in an intense environment.

When you reach what appears to be final agreement, 'summarise your understanding of the situation and write it down. Sometimes you can say, ' I will get this typed up this afternoon; however, I have the key points written out here. Can we photocopy these and initial them before I leave?' If he says, 'Yes', which is the normal response at this point, we have absolute clarity and agreement on the terms. If he hesitates, we can clear up any misunderstanding and ensure we reach agreement before we leave.

One of my clients selling computers had secured what they thought was an agreed deal with a major bank: an initial delivery worth in the region of £100,000. The order form had been made up in the name of my client and had been verbally agreed by the bank, with the paperwork promised. My client represented two major PC manufacturers – international household names – and in good faith told the unsuccessful supplier that the deal was going to their competitor unless they could do something better.

The salesman went on holiday. When he came back the PC manufacturer had gone in with slightly used models and had secured the deal unethically. Agreement should have been firmer, he thought he had the deal. In reality it was not as clear cut as he imagined it to be. He should have made certain that agreement was unequivocally in place.

Introductory Concepts

Way 14 The quandary of uncertainty

Negotiation is inherent in human nature and with it a sense of uncertainty. That's one of the reasons why Britons particularly dislike the process. Many of us would far rather prices, proposals and terms were fixed in every way, so that we could ask for what we want, and make a decision based purely on our perception of value. What causes this quandary?

Simply everything is unknown. I don't know what a 'good' deal is in this case. Is the other person ripping me off? What will my peers, my family, my boss think of the agreement I have reached? Could I have got a better deal in some way? All this produces stress, unease, uncertainty.

As I write this the British government faces this quandary of uncertainty with BSE or Mad Cow Disease. They don't know whether to cull thousands or millions of cattle. They don't know how much the EU will cough up in compensation for culling or how much they will have to ask the British taxpayer to pay. For that reason they find it difficult to decide where to start in their negotiating process.

In many cases, we really do not know what price to start at. Many times we will not know for sure if we could have got more. We may never know if we could have persuaded our counterpart to move further. That is the reality of many of the negotiations with which we are involved.

Way 15 Avoid intransigence

The easy way out is an offer or price from which we refuse to budge. It removes the indecision. It removes the risk of causing offence, it removes the risk of getting it wrong. However, we should always expect a competent business-man to offer less than we ask for. Putting it another way, it is very rare in my experience for a potential customer to say, 'This is fantastic, please let me pay more than you are asking'.

I have four children and I know that negotiation is a natural part of their behaviour. Joshua has just been given extra chores for which he has had an increase in his pocket money. This week he came back and said this £1 is not enough for the extra work. The trouble is we have become dependent on his work. And he is doing a very good job. Now I can make a decision from which I refuse to budge. But if I do that, I lose Joshua's willing co-operation. So negotiation is inevitable.

Over many years I have been responsible for purchasing cars appropriate to our image in the market. Two makes suited our requirements — Volvo and BMW. For years BMW dealers would take a stance of intransigence from which they would not shift. In other words, they would not negotiate. In every case I bought Volvo because BMW would not negotiate on price, service or extras. Last year BMW did begin to negotiate and they got my business for the first time in seven years; they could have had it much sooner by avoiding intransigence.

One of my friends is currently finance director for a major international distribution company. They conducted a sales presentation which they won for distribution services with a national chain. Before the contract was ratified the national chain was subject to a take-over and the new parent simply renewed the contract with the existing supplier.

The following year both companies were pitched against each other. My friend's company was in many ways the better choice and probably the preferred supplier. They were asked to review their set up costs. This included items such as training and software implementation. Fairly soft costs. But company policy was essentially intransigent. They simply would not budge on those costs. The other supplier offered them totally free and got the business.

To the casual observer it may appear that price was the issue. The reality was that intransigence was the issue. When my friend evaluated the cost of the set-up compared with the net profit over even the first year the difference was minuscule.

My friend put it this way, 'Being obsessed with short-term profitability led us to miss the whole deal. It stopped us from seeing the supplier's point of view and wasted enormous amounts of time spent in preparation and presentation'. Intransigence may remove some uncertainty. But it will always cost us.

Way 16 Understand aspiration

Most companies that go bankrupt, as we well know, are usually busy. They were just busy doing the wrong things but, more importantly, on the wrong terms. The competitive free market economy puts a downward pressure on our aspirations.

Human nature and the free market economy also inspire positive aspiration. The combination affects what we aim for, what we expect to get and what we would ideally like to achieve. The skilled buyer understands this and will use a routine tactic. When we give our price this buyer rarely says 'Fantastic, how reasonable!' No! He says, 'What? How much?' When he does that, or when he tells us that our competitors' prices are much lower, what is the impact? His technique forces us to lower our aspirations. We tend to lower them, and lower our price.

The reverse should be true. For that reason negotiation is not for the few, it is for every responsible businessman or woman. Everyone of us wanting to achieve increased profit will need to face negotiation with a brave heart and a sound approach. Our first response is to defend our aspiration consistently.

Way 17 Never say yes first time

Of all the principles we shall look at, this one is the simplest and probably the most effective. Remembering this will save you money and increase your profit on every single deal you make. This principle should be a reflex action.

I was co-presenting at a seminar in a large room at Heathrow. One of the other presenters asked the delegates this question, 'How many of you here *never* pay the full rate for hotel rooms?' About one-third of the room raised their hands. That means two thirds were regularly paying too much for overnight stays.

A friend of mine was staying away in a hotel to prepare for a new seminar he was writing. The hotel was one of a nationally recognised and reputable chain, located in Milton Keynes. He simply asked, 'What is your best rate?' and managed to negotiate from an offered rate of £120 down to £78 per night. Never say yes first time.

What about when you buy advertising? Did you know that you should never pay the full rate? Agencies usually claim 10 per cent so you can use that fact to get 10 per cent reduction straight away. Call some advertisers to see what response they have achieved, and use that information to lower the magazine's aspiration. You can even send a cheque for half the rate, and say, 'Feel free to cash my cheque when you place my advert on the inside back cover'.

Way 18 What we think conditions our approach

The other person in a negotiation often exercises more authority, not because he has it in reality, but simply because he thinks he has it. We can make this worse by allowing ourselves to believe that our counterpart has more strength than he has. When we do that, we compound the strength he already feels.

Your counterpart, whoever he is, can appear more powerful. Maybe because you feel insecure. Perhaps because he has the ability to pay you or supply something you badly need. The reality is often the reverse: he needs what you can offer, the problems you can overcome, the opportunities you can create, the obstacles you can remove, the preferences you can satisfy.

We must build and enhance our authority in negotiation. How you see it determines your outcome. The old adage, 'Seeing is believing' applies here. Authority and confidence stem from our own perception. The authority you carry in a negotiation is largely based on your confidence. It is a reflection of your state of mind but it is real and has real effect on the outcome.

Confidence is a key. If you lose your own confidence the counterpart will intuitively pick that up and you will end the negotiation in a much weaker position than you need to. Tactics therefore need to be clear before you go into the negotiation. Lose the confidence of your counterpart and you overstep the mark. You won't regain the high ground.

Authority comes from confidence. Our sources of confidence come from the preparation phase. Thinking through all the advantages we have to offer, thinking through all the gaps in the weaknesses of the other person. We strengthen our mind and strengthen our position. To aid us in this process we need to assess and build our authority.

Enhance your Authority

Way 19 The authority of print

There is a real authority in having prices, costs and details in print. Printed material carries an inherent believability. If you are a buyer you may choose to have target prices, or competitive prices, or last year's prices. You may have a printed page detailing the implications of proposed prices and their impact on profit, on staffing levels etc. You may even have a summary business plan built on your ability to achieve a given price for this contract. It is so simple but so effective it intimidates the seller into a defensive posture.

For consultants or others selling professional services, what often happens for example is that you quote a daily fee of £200 or £2000 and the buyer has nothing to measure it against. How does he know that this is in fact legitimate? How does he know that you haven't made this figure up? How does he know that you are not just 'trying it on'? Having it in print makes it appear credible, more believable and more legitimate.

Either side of the negotiating table having printed material disarms the other person. It makes it more difficult for them to squeeze more out of the deal. Printed price lists, letters from superiors, letters from current customers or suppliers, departmental budgets, letters from your superior, standard forms, articles from newspapers, competitors' brochures — all these have the power of authority for you to use. If you don't have any material preprinted then produce it on your own word processor with a date and a reference to give it validity.

Whatever printed material you deem appropriate in a particular negotiation, use it to validate your apparently limited ability to move from a desired position. It makes it harder for the other person to ask you for any form of concession and it will build your confidence for the position you are taking. If the tactic is being used on you, one response is to say, 'Actually, that is not relevant to this particular application'. It doesn't always work but it does buy you some time!

Ed is a computer guru. He was telling me last week how he went to a High Street outlet and bought a joystick. The joysticks were on sale for £80; he saw a slightly damaged unit and bargained for it at £65. When he tried it out, it was faulty so he took it back and asked for cash back, and a receipt clearly marked with the model on it. They had no others in stock so he went to another store where the unit was on sale for £90. He produced his receipt for £65, and asked them if they could match the price which they did. His printed receipt was a source of authority.

Way 20 The authority of information

Here we must take the time and make the effort to collect as much information as we can about the other side and their organisation.

'W' questions are the method: what, which, when, why, who and how? Too often, busy professional people talk rather than listen. The classic example is when you get an enquiry, on an incoming telephone call. The prospect has found your name in a directory. Let's say he calls and says, 'Can you tell me about your training facilities?'

We answer we've got ropes, we've got camping facilities, we've got safety certification, we've got brilliant instructors, we've got acres of land, we've got, we've got, we've got! What we've actually got is, no power, no negotiation strength and no real perception of his requirements. Worst of all we have given him a load of information about ourselves and further weakened our position.

When he says, 'Can you tell me about your training facilities' – the reply should be 'Certainly, my name is . . . Who am I speaking to? And your company name? To enable me to get back to you, may I have your telephone number?' Before I tell you could I ask you? And then we move into our power-enriching W questions:

- What are you looking to achieve from your training?

- How have you used outdoor training before?

- How many participants?

- What previous training have they had?

- What are their responsibilities in the company or the team?

- What particularly are you looking for in the successful provider?

- What difficulties have you experienced with previous suppliers?

That is the key question. It will often expose real need or weakness and will give you a significant point of authority.
Stay in tight control of the flow of information to the other party about your organisation. Take great care in exposing your needs, your dependency, staff shortages, cost break-downs. The only information we should give the other party is the advantage, the gain, the benefit. Which is why we must ask the W questions.

W questions enable us to uncover what the other person really needs and wants. If we are selling they enable us to discover with accuracy which unique selling point (USP) is relevant, meaningful and powerful. If you think you have a 'cure all' USP which in reality is not meaningful or relevant to this buyer, it is clearly not a unique perceived benefit at all.

Whether you are buying or selling you have the freedom to be silent. Don't be under pressure to answer every ques-tion. You don't have to talk. Often, if you don't respond to the other person's comment or question, he will speak after a short, sometimes uncomfortable wait. In that situation your counterpart may give away more information. Information that he intended to keep from you. Don't be unduly con-cerned by apparently embarrassing silences.

Because of your silence you will learn more and more, which is to your advantage in the negotiation. Also, remain-ing silent for a while gives you more time to think, more time to decide on your next move.

Way 21 The authority of patience

Rush equals loss. There is often pressure to agree a deal, to close the sale or make the purchase. The tyranny of the urgent shouts so loudly that we don't give time to uncover information.

Just last week I received a call from an electronics company wanting what they said was a marketing review. I was pressurised with work load, I told them I don't do speculative visits. I made some assumptions from a rushed conversation about what they were really looking for. I then put together a proposal, equally rushed, and made a subsequent follow-up call.

During the follow-up call it became clear that my rush had resulted in three damaging things. First, I had obtained inadequate information about them and their requirements. Second, I voluntarily printed a cost breakdown, which I shouldn't have done and from which they immediately negotiated. Third, my overall proposal was weak because I had not focused on the key points. I had totally missed the USP and I am currently on an uphill struggle to regain my lost ground. All that because I was in too much of a hurry.

What about time pressures on the buyer? When you are buying you can usually build in time to allow to you to negotiate from maximum strength. The longer you can keep the salesman waiting for an answer the more likely he is to concede, to give things away that he would not otherwise have given. The more relaxed you are about the buying process the more pressure it exerts on the seller.

Bide your time and wait for that moment where your counterpart expresses weakness. Wait until your opposite number is vulnerable, look for that moment and then move in.

One of my clients has a specialist skill in the buying and selling of businesses. The key, he told me, lies in timing. Knowing the right time is the critical factor in both buying and selling. There are all kinds of reasons why an individual might sell his company. He might be near retiring age with no family to pass the business on to. The business may need to move on, and he may not have the resource or the infrastructure to do it. But even when these needs are clear, you have to wait and be patient.

I have watched it myself, particularly with sole traders, you negotiate and think the time is right but they pull back at the last minute. Not as a tactic, simply out of uncertainty. If you try to pressurise them, you nearly always frighten them off. Patience is what you need. Sometimes it can take years. You may come close to agreement several times with the uncertain party backing off several times. It is normal, and if you want to succeed you must prepare yourself for this inevitable delay.

The party who is most compelled by time is weaker — plan to have time, build in time.

Way 22 The authority of positive posturing

All the pressures on us both buyer and seller are downward as far as price is concerned. We need to stop the rot and build value, build authority, build confidence.

This is not mind over matter. This is stark reality. For sellers, your own thoughts and the negative environment which so often surrounds you, mean that you go into negotiation already feeling that your prices are too high. In fact it is amusingly uncommon to meet a salesman who believes his prices are low or right. Any buyer worth his salt is going to try to make you feel that even more keenly.

One of the things that can be hard for salesmen is that in nearly every application more people say 'No' than 'Yes'. There is nothing wrong with that. A good salesman may secure one sale in every three to four appointments. He should likely be proud of that achievement. However, his mind has been told 'No' more than 'Yes' . Let's say he does 100 appointments per month. That means 75 people or companies have said 'No' and only 25 have said 'Yes'. As a sales manager I would probably be pleased with that performance and rightly so. But what of the effect on the salesman's state of mind? I was listening to a sales trainer recently in Canada who insisted that all his salesmen had 20 'No's per week — otherwise they didn't get paid!

Whatever our job it can condition us to go into negotiation in a negative frame of mind. Working environments often bring us into contact with criticism and complaints. We hear negative things so often we begin to believe them. These negative inputs can weigh us down. If we are not careful our motivation and determination can drown under their weight.

Skilled negotiators spend time building up their own confidence, making sure before any significant negotiation that they feel good about the process and their role in it, objectively restating to themselves the positive value of this deal, this agreement, and their impact on it. It often helps to write down key positive statements about the project, the product the deal and its effect. Doing this is cathartic, it begins to wash clean those negative stains and provides a clean fresh edge to our motivation and performance.

Way 23 The authority of leverage

Let me suggest three levers. The primary lever in the negotiation is your USP that we have already looked at in some detail. Your product or service, the company, you the person. In 20 years of negotiation, the USP has always been the primary key for increased profit, better deals and greater profit: the primary key to increasing power and increasing confidence. If we don't have or are unclear about our USPs our power is fundamentally weakened.

Distance is another lever. Distance retains strength: if we are weaker meet them, if we are stronger don't meet them. I was recently tying up a deal with an international author and seminar presenter. I had quoted £5200 for a particular package and I was sent a message by his office manager (via his car phone) saying the deal could go ahead if we could agree £5000. He was a buyer with significant strength and he retained it by using the distance. I couldn't contact him personally and he used that fact cleverly.

The third lever is 'fallback'. Fallback means I have a good or acceptable alternative to agreement being negotiated. The easier we can walk away from the negotiating environment, the better our result.

If you need the deal more than you can cope with losing it, you will be less authoritative in the negotiation. If there is real pressure on you to secure this one at all costs, it will affect the outcome negatively, particularly if you believe there is little pressure on your counterpart to do the same.

Way 24 The authority of resolved weaknesses

In nearly every negotiation both parties have concealed areas of weakness. If our counterpart is effective he will hunt these areas out and exploit them. So he should! How can he do that with such apparent ease? If we don't deal with our areas of exposure or weakness he will sense uncertainty and he will chase it until the weakness is exposed. He will then rightly use that to strengthen his own position. Our own attention is then focused inevitably on the exposed weakness and we are left in a defensive state trying to limit whatever damage is now being done.

The answer lay with us all along. The fact is we probably knew the weakness existed and even if our counterpart had not raised it, it was busy undermining our confidence and eroding our authority.

The way to handle this is to put some time aside, list all the elements of your business that are relevant to any negotiation. In one column detail all the strengths, in another, list any weaknesses you can think of. Simply thinking through those weaknesses and listing them, facing them head on, can be of great value. That process on its own can often yield some obvious answers. It may even solve some niggling business problems for you. But the real goal is to turn them into positive attributes or strengths. At the very least be totally confident in your own ability to deal with any purported weakness in the negotiation. Be confident in your own method of handling it in the process.

Tactics and Countermeasures

In any negotiation, tactics are regularly brought into play. It is vital that we know the most common ones. It is equally vital that we know how to counter if they are used on us in the process. If we are in buying mode we can try these tactics or some variant of them. If we are in selling mode we can learn ways to respond appropriately when these tactics are used on us, as they invariably will be.

Knowing and therefore identifying any tactic takes the emotion out of the system. It frees your mind to think about the countermeasures — ways to deal efficiently with the tactic.

These tactics often appear as non-negotiable issues but in fact rarely are!

Way 25 Aspiration lowering

How does the other person attempt to lower our aspirations on price? There are two commonly applied tactics. The first is to compare your offer with your competitors' terms or product. The second is a straightforward request.

Comparing your offer

Cost	They are cheaper.
Delivery	They can do the audit ten days sooner.
Quantity	They are providing sample letters, adverts and telesales scripts.
New Features	They provide a 60 day helpline.
Security	They guarantee our taxation liability, they guarantee safety.
Payment	They allow 90 days for payment.

Straightforward request

Here the other person may use a tricky phrase,' At this point it is our company policy to agree suppliers' discount level' or 'It is normal business practice in these cases to agree supplier discount.'

Price is a legitimate and obvious target in any negotiation and every sensible buyer should try it. The phrase,'It is normal business practice ' is clever, it can easily catch you out. It can subtly put pressure on you to conform to what is being declared as normal. We should never succumb to the pressure to drop our price.

The first line of counterattack is to ask 'Why?' You can put it in a statement like this, 'You are suggesting that our price is too high. Can I ask too high in relation to what?'

What is the reason for asking a question like that? Simply that our counterpart's attempt to rot our price could mean any one of these:

- More expensive than I thought

- I want a discount

- This is more than I can sanction

- Somebody else is cheaper

- I am not yet convinced of the value

- This is actually outside our budget.

Understanding the real reason behind the challenge to our price enables us to respond appropriately. We then trade; in other words nothing at all is ever given away. Any ultimate adjustment in price must always be exchanged for something else from our counterpart.

A pre-emptive countermeasure to this tactic is to ask for more in the first place. Buyer or seller — ask for more, you get more. Aiming higher gives us room to negotiate. It means giving yourself more room to make concessions, it means that we don't keep eroding company margins.

The price, however, must be realistic and perceived to be legitimate. We can expect our counterpart to challenge anything that looks artificially high — we must have good reasons. If he thinks we are trying it on he will have a cynical view of the rest of our negotiations that will prove most unhelpful, and jeopardise future business.

A further practical countermeasure is to stop, then slowly and deliberately use a calculator to see the real costs of conceding to price challenges. Let your opponent see you using it, too. Multiply by the number of clients, number of days per year, so that both you and he see the real impact of any concession. It also shows that you have done your homework and that you have legitimate reasons for defending that price.

Way 26 It's all I have got

Your house is ideally situated and my wife and I like the area, but you want £110,000 and with our deposit and the maximum we can borrow, the most we can find is £90,000 — it's all I've got . . .

The implication is a positive attitude towards us and our proposal but an implied limit to the funds available. A normal but wrong response is to offer discount. A good negotiator must have another proposal available. Any change to price must mean a change to the terms. If we are required to change the price we must insist that they accept changes to the proposal or elements of it.

Suggesting a changed proposal will test whether our counterpart has genuinely limited funds. If he is not interested, he is simply trying it on. The simple countermeasure is to offer an alternative:

- Offer changed methods of payment.
- Offer a change to the service, eg instead of two days we could redesign the course into one longer day.
- Offer to change the whole package in some way, eg the helpline, the printed report, the briefing session conducted by telephone rather than by visit etc.
- Offer changed volumes, changed delivery dates.

The key is any change on price must accompany change in the proposal, otherwise we give away what we should never give away.

I mentioned earlier how one of my recent clients used his strength by keeping his distance, and dealing with me through his office manager. You recall he was asking me to reduce my proposal by £200. I was frustrated, I was busy, I was tired and someone was lowering my aspirations. It would be so easy to rationalise away £200. But £200 × 10 clients per month × 10 months is £20,000. That is a lot of money. So I changed the proposal. I said we will agree to £5000 but it means reducing the number of hours available on the telephone helpline and we require payment on the day.

A different price required a different proposal and we both settled happily for that.

Way 27 The hurdle

Countless times I have been in a negotiation and the other person has said 'You must be joking' or ' You will have to improve that'. They might say, 'You are getting close — *but!*' That, by the way, always means ' Your price is high and it's a *hurdle* to the agreement. Drop the hurdle and let's see what we can do'.

They are implying that price is the key issue and other elements of the negotiation are acceptable. Turn it to your advantage. Your immediate response should be something like this, From what you are saying, 'it seems that are you are happy with the proposal. If we can agree together on price can I assume we have a deal?'

What we are doing here is using the other person's ploy to our advantage, narrowing down any possible further areas of potential disagreement.

Don't catch price rot! Performance is part of our price and we must communicate that. A carefully crafted approach would go like this, 'Let me ask you, isn't it true that all companies have a choice to make? They can either provide a service which does just as much as possible for their customers, or they can provide a service which does just enough to get by with. Isn't that the choice that every company must make?' The other person usually says,'Yes'. We say, 'Well, what would you prefer from us, as much as possible or just enough to get by with?'

We can do better on price if you accept the following. If we have to trade we do so reluctantly. We make sure that any movement on our side is accompanied by movement on their side.

Way 28 The A-team factor

When my two sons were younger, our favourite joint viewing was *The A-Team*. One speciality would be when a hapless victim would be interrogated by 'Mr T', a big and frightening individual, together with 'Face' who was always ' Mr Nice'. Mr T would always scowl, growl, threaten and bully. Face would then come and gently, quietly, offer a way out, 'If only you would talk'. He would offer a drink, offer kindness, offer much nicer sounding alternatives. Nearly every time the victim would be conned. He would give in unnecessarily.

The same tactic is applied in negotiation. The buyer brings in his financial director who sourly pulls your proposal to pieces. He gets angry with your prices and may even raise his voice to you. After a while he gets called into another meeting.

The buyer turns round to you like an old friend. He apologises for his director and offers much more reasonable sounding terms. That is danger time! Beware of his tactic because it seems so reasonable, but only in comparison with the bully. The bully has set us up for Mr Nice who then seems reasonable. The problem is because we have been deflated and our aspirations have been lowered we can too quickly negotiate from the wrong base.

The best possible thing you can do is laugh when you spot the tactic. Lower their authority by showing them you know what they are doing. Then don't negotiate immediately otherwise you will be comparing the reasonable buyers' demands with the bully. Instead excuse yourself, give yourself time, take a loo break and take time to compare current demands with what you had already determined as your negotiating position.

Way 29 Erosion

My family and I visited a famous model village in the Isle of Wight. It was situated on a cliff top — right on the edge —

with spectacular views over the Atlantic Ocean. A few days after we visited the place, it shut down because erosion from the constant pounding of the sea had eaten away at its foundations. Some of the exhibits had slipped into the sea — lost for ever. Erosion is often not taken seriously. In negotiation we can make it work well for us.

Our counterpart has fixed terms or amounts or fixed prices. We keep eroding away at the edges, trying to make his firm stance give way. This is a marvellously effective tactic, which I try to use as routinely as I can. It works by using a simple question, 'If I buy this, will you throw in that?' I was buying some suits recently. I let it be known that I was interested in buying one suit. I asked,' If I buy three, what discount will you give and how many shirts and ties will you throw in ?' Whenever you are in buying mode try to use this tactic.

If you are selling, beware because the buyer wants to get some little extras. These are dangerous because they often appear small, but multiplied they have a profound effect. We must price them, identify their real cost and be seen to be doing it. We must never give in to the eroding tactic. We must trade, not give in.

Let's say we are in property or estate agency. We offer to sell a house for 2.5 per cent commission. The owner wants to negotiate to 2 per cent. The value of the house is £200,000. Half a per cent. Doesn't sound very much does it? In reality it is a great deal: 2 per cent is £4000, 2.5 per cent is £5000. It means I am losing 20 per cent of my income and probably a much higher percentage of profit. If I make five similar sales each month, I am losing £5000 per month, £60,000 per year.

Look at it in another light. If five houses per month at 2.5 per cent yields £80,000 profit each year, then that half per cent will reduce my profit from £80,000 to just £20,000. That half per cent has reduced my profit by a staggering 75 per cent.

I am often asked for training manuals. Say a buyer asks me for 100 extra training manuals — gently eroding my determination! I calculate how much that costs, possibly £5 each, and say incredulously, 'You are asking me to give away £500. I do five of these events each month; you are suggesting I give away £2500 each month, that's £30,000 each year'.

It's calculator time again. Get out the calculator and let him see you do the sums, talk out loud while you do it, and make sure that the outcome is spoken out and ideally written down in front of the other party. It helps to let the other person see your calculations and your cost implications. Let him see on paper the calculation you have just made.

Way 30 The upward spiral

Have you ever climbed the spiral stairs of a lighthouse or some other tall building? I remember doing this with my children on several occasions. You think you are there, and then someone tells you there is more to climb! Unless you are really motivated that extra upward effort can prove too much and you succumb to the downward pressure of gravity and your clinging children. The upward spiral in negotiation feels similar. You are sure you have reached the end and then your counterpart seems to have started all over again. It is very wearing and that is its danger.

This can be used by both buyer and seller. We may have agreed in principle but then the other person lets time pass to lower our aspirations and does not send in the signed order form or does not ratify the agreement and then finds some way of starting the negotiation all over again.

I have seen this happen time and time again with sales people. A salesman makes a sale and thinks he has agreed the terms. He tells his sales manager that they have a verbal agreement and they count it in the current month's sales figures. A few days before the end of the month the signed order form has not appeared. Suddenly now the sales manager is faced with a dilemma. He just has to have that business, because he has committed himself to the month's result. When he calls the prospective customer, the urgency will be clearly audible in his approach. The buyer will see the date, put two and two together and press for a better deal. In nearly every case the salesman or his manager will end up giving too much away.

As a means of using the upward spiral, it is a useful tactic for buyers to probe to find out from the salesman what pressures are on him or his company to meet monthly or quarterly figures. Ask the seller how his commission scheme operates, ask what figures are important to his company this month or this quarter. I used this tactic for one of my clients. I was negotiating on their behalf for some office equipment. We had secured some good deals but were unhappy with the proposal on fax machines. My client sends and receives over 100,000 faxes each year and we needed some robust, fast machines with specific functions. We approached the key suppliers, found some appropriate models and began to negotiate.

I knew which model we wanted, but could not achieve my target price. I did not want to pay for at least three months and my client could wait for delivery. The salesman was convinced he had the sale in the bag, so I stalled. I began asking the salesman about his own development within the company, his career, his commission. From those questions I discovered that within one month he would be moving to another department. He needed to surpass a threshold figure, after which any sales brought in this month would be allowable as part of the commission scheme for his new job. My purchase could help him achieve that threshold.

I suggested that he take my proposal back to head office. My proposal was to buy at my target price. I would place the order now, and give him three post-dated cheques on the spot. He came back one day later and the deal was agreed.

Another variation is where buyer or seller may use the upward spiral by passing final decision, or 'Written approval' further and further up the management scale. In other words, they make it appear that they are not authorised to agree these 'additional points' — it must be referred to their superior. By inference if we will drop these new requests or proposed changes they can still make the agreement. Call their bluff. They may be just as unwilling to start again as we are. You might start closing up your briefcase and say, 'I am sorry if we can't approve what I thought we had agreed. It may be that my MD will have to start discussions again with your boss'. It is usually enough, it is phrased in such a way that he can backtrack without losing face.

Upward spiral after agreement does sometimes happen even though it is unethical. I had a variation of this dirty trick played on me yesterday. I was out with my family and some friends taking a walk in the New Forest. We stopped for afternoon tea in a tea room and placed our order. We ordered tea to drink for four, three sodas and then asked for five scones with cream and jam. The proprietor said rather quickly, 'You want five cream teas?' We nodded assent without thinking.

You can guess the rest! The five cream teas included vast quantities of scones plus cakes which we had not asked for. The price was of course far higher than the cost of five scones with cream and jam. It left a nasty taste in our mouths, not because we would have minded the proprietor trying to up-sell our order, but because it had been done in an underhand manner. The terms had been escalated unethically.

Sometimes if a buyer does that to us, we can call his bluff again by saying that we can no longer do it for the original price and give him a new one. Then he has to negotiate all over again and may well be content to settle at the original price.

Way 31 This is not negotiable

When a buyer uses this tactic he might say, 'I have talked to my superiors, we have checked prices with your competitors, and this is all we are prepared to pay'. Or he might say, 'Don't give me your benefit story, we know what we are doing, this is our bottom line'. When a seller uses the same tactic he might simply say, 'That is not negotiable'. Neither seller or buyer should use these phrases because they usually produce anger and they show poor negotiating skills. When the buyer uses these phrases the great temptation is to cave in to price.

One of my friends worked as salesman for a professional European consulting service. Their company policy meant that in most cases the seller would say, 'We do not negotiate' and would in fact walk away from the sale rather than do a deal. I understand their determination to hold on to price and not erode profits. However, one in two of those that walked away, could have been saved with a gesture which would enable them to save face.

You could say in a situation like that, 'Company policy does not enable me to offer any kind of discount, however, if you . . . then we . . .' Maybe you could offer a small PC based software for him to develop your service, or a manual, or a reference book. There has to be a way for him to save face.

When our counterpart uses this phrase we have two options; we either succumb to pressure on price, or handle it. If we are to handle it we must give him a face-saving way out otherwise we produce deadlock. We can say, for example 'I would like to take it but it's just not possible. However, if you could do this . . . we could do that . . .'.

If a buyer says, 'Is your fee negotiable?' we say, 'We are happy to listen to any constructive suggestions you may have about the overall proposal'. My company was approached recently, and I was asked to be a keynote speaker at a business conference in Milton Keynes. I quoted my fee, and there was a telling silence. The other person began to negotiate, suggesting that I might like to do the seminar free, in return for a number of business opportunities. When I made it clear that it was not really of interest, he asked the next obvious question, 'Is your fee negotiable?' My answer was straightforward, 'I'm happy to look at this constructively — one of my colleagues would be interested in the business opportunities, he is prepared to come and speak and the cost will be significantly lower'. He got a lower price but he had to take a different proposal.

It is worth negotiating, worth hanging in there, and if we give him a face-saving way out our opposite number will either back off or moderate his approach, if he sees that we legitimately defend our price.

Don't ever assume that anything is not negotiable. A friend of mine was relating a particular customs raid. The ship was boarded at Tilbury and was being checked for illegally distilled spirit. Apparently on some voyages the practice of one or two crew members is to use denatured spirit, add fruit or potatoes, boil it, strain it and serve it up!

On this particular ship the offending distiller assumed he was going to be apprehended and instead of pouring it overboard he drank the lot. He was violently ill and subsequently died with over 18 times the safe limit in his blood. Tragic and in every sense unnecessary. But he assumed the outcome was not negotiable, with dire consequences.

Way 32 What ifs

What if we treble our requirement? What if we could give a two year agreement? As soon as our opponent uses phrases like this he is able to discover any slack in our price or in our approach and he will negotiate from it.

I travel a great deal in the Third World and love to sharpen my skills in street market negotiation. The principles are just the same. You can try them in your local antique shop. Having browsed around and shown a general interest, point to two items and say, 'I'm interested in your best price, what if I take both?' The answer comes back, 'One thousand pounds'. Point to the one you don't want and say, ' How much just for that one?' He says, ' Six-hundred'. You say, 'Fine, I'll have the other one for £400.' You have established some slack, and created room for negotiation.

My eldest son and I are negotiating to buy shot-gun cartridges. We ask one dealer 'How much if we buy them by the box?' He replies, 'fifteen pence each'. We say what if we buy 1000?' He replies, 'Twelve pence each'. We then ask, 'How many do you have in stock?' He replies, 'Twenty thousand'. We say, 'What if we buy half your stock?' He says, 'Ten pence each'.

As the buyers, we have now established significant slack in what he charges. One thing is for certain, whatever price we get, we won't be paying 15p each. Any time you use this tactic as a buyer, you will of course discover slack in the price and you should negotiate from it. If you are the seller experiencing this tactic then as a general rule don't shoot from the hip. Buy time and get back the control, by asking 'W' questions. Ask about his application, identify any problems or constraints or obstacles that he may be encountering. Check on his time constraints, ask what it is that he is most concerned with. Ask about safety, cost savings in fuel efficiency, whatever you can ask. Ask what difficulties he has experienced with previous supply. Most importantly, ask what his usage is. A good way to do that is to ask in the past tense, such as, 'What was your monthly consumption last year?'

From time to time, our counterpart will ask for a price breakdown. If he does, we may have to give it, but we should never be pressurised into pricing on the spot. Come back with a price when we have carefully thought through the implications. Price things they can do low. Things that only we can do, price them high. Don't be bound by tramlines of method that you have used in the past. But also be willing to stick by your revealed pricing method if he wants to adjust his total requirement.

Just last week I priced a marketing audit for a prospect. In my price I include a sum for both myself and one of my senior clinicians to do the brief together and jointly to write the plan. The same senior clinician is included in the price to provide helpline duties for 90 days. He also conducts tele-sales coaching immediately after the plan is presented.

The prospect understandably asked me to consider doing the audit alone, bringing in the senior clinician for the tele-sales work only. Because his rate is significantly lower than mine I was able to demonstrate that taking him out of the briefing session would save a minuscule amount, for two reasons. First, he would now have to conduct a briefing session of his own for the telesales coaching. Second the helpline content would dramatically *increase* in price because I would have to take that responsibility. The saving for the prospect was a few hundred pounds and the loss of input would far outweigh the minimal saving available. The prospect saw it immediately.

Way 33 Deadlines

The other person can put a time deadline into the negotiation to try and pressure us into accepting lower terms than we would otherwise have done.

If you are on the receiving end, don't just accept stated deadlines — negotiate them. Many of us do it all the time for example, with hotel rooms. Just about every hotel, for example, requires that you vacate your bedroom by 12 noon. They put it into print, trying to enhance their authority. I rarely leave before 2 pm, often later than that, without paying any extra. You might say, 'I'm meeting some customers here for lunch — using your facilities — I want to be able to change for a meeting shortly after that, I need to use my bedroom until then; I assume that is okay?'

As I write this chapter I have just left the Toronto Sheraton having conducted a seminar. I checked out at 3.45 instead of 12 noon simply by saying this, 'I ran two seminars here yesterday, would you please be gracious and extend my check out time until 4 o'clock?' They wanted me to leave by 3pm so I settled finally by leaving at 3.45.

A buyer can use deadlines like these:

- 'Engineering insist that we agree this order by the weekend'.

- 'My boss has to approve and I have a meeting scheduled with him for final signature in 30 minutes'.

- 'It's now or never — we either agree right away or I will look elsewhere'.

- 'Our client has insisted that we agree better terms from our suppliers this week'.

What should the seller do in response? He should never accept the apparent urgency of the deadline and should always test it. 'I appreciate the importance of this to you but we will need four more days — I assume we can find a way round that?' If having tested the deadline it is real and immovable, you can still respond and save face by asking to call your office for confirmation.

There are some deadlines the seller can use either to preempt or counter this particular tactic:

- 'Our offer only lasts this week.'

- 'Cost of materials increases this month which means the price goes up on 1 February.'

- 'If we don't agree to proceed by 1 February then we cannot produce the report by the end of February.'

Negotiable Variables – or Tradeable Concessions

So far we have looked in different ways at the first four of our six key elements — prepare, rehearse, describe, propose. Now we turn to the heart of all successful negotiation and that is the bargaining phase. Remember our definition, 'To bargain means to make it a condition of an agreement that something should be done'.

Bargaining means making any move on your part *conditional* on a move from your opposite number. There should never be any exception to this rule. It should be indelibly imprinted into our minds. Concessions must be traded with care. In simple terms we never give assent to any concession until the other person has agreed what he will give in return.

Unskilled negotiators find a pressure to move quickly to give things away. If your counterpart has any sense he will ask you for more and the likelihood is that he will keep asking.

Way 34 Never give, always trade

Never give something away without working out what it means to them. Never give something away without getting something back. And always make what we give seem valuable or significant.

Never give, always trade. What I offer you, must be balanced by what you offer me. Nothing is given away. If we move on any term we must ensure that the other person moves towards us. Putting this into practice will automatically make you feel more authoritative. It will give you increasing confidence, and as you practise, it will quickly yield improving results.

Way 35 Trade what is cheap to you

Trade what is cheap to you and what is valuable to him. We must know the cost to us of any concession we make. We should know which things we can offer or trade that cost very little to us but which could be of high value to our opposite number.

Think this through carefully. Ask yourself, 'If I give this, what obstacle does it overcome, how much would that save?' Ask, 'What opportunity does this create for him or his company, what financial benefit could that bring to him?' 'What preference does this satisfy? What problem does this solve?' We ask ourselves what is this worth to him in savings, in productivity, in financial terms. The more specific we can be about the gain to the other party, the more valuable what we have to trade will appear to him.

One tradeable we can build in, which can cost us very little, is some form of guarantee. Guarantees often have high perceived value to the other person and yet may well cost us nothing. Let me illustrate. Most of the seminars I run have an unconditional 'Money back' guarantee. If you are not totally satisfied with the value gained we will refund your fees in full. In 15 years of training hardly ever has someone asked for their money back, so the guarantee has cost me nothing but has high validity to a prospective delegate or host client company.

A variation of this technique was used by one of my associate companies offering colour sales brochures. They would guarantee a minimum level of sales enquiries from these brochures, provided that they were used in a specific way with supporting documentation. They sold hundreds of brochures and telesales commissions. Not one company ever came back having failed to achieve the guaranteed result. But that was not the point, the point was the guarantee had high perceived confidence and security value to the buyer. Was it low cost or low risk? Yes. In the unlikely event of any customer not achieving the promised levels of business one of the company's many telesales staff would get on the phone for a few hours and generate the promised level of enquiries. As a side effect it was a marvellous way to back-sell the telesales operation.

Ask yourself what guarantees what you could offer as part of your negotiation process. Guarantees that are low cost and low risk to us, but high value to the other party. The technique applies equally when we are in the buying mode. What can we guarantee as a buyer? For example; 'We are prepared to consider three years' repeat purchase subject to your company remaining competitive and your quality staying consistently at our Ship To Stock Standard. If we could agree to that, we would expect the following from you . . . '. Remember, never give, always trade.

One of my associates was selling PC Notebooks to hotel chains on a 'Roll-out' programme. At six to seven venues, these notebooks had to be delivered on the previous night, to the host hotel, configured in batches of eight to ten. The customer was negotiating hard on price. My associate used the guarantee as part of her concession trading, 'We can't adjust the price but what we can do is to have a technician at the hotel the previous night, taking responsibility for the security of the PCs. He will ensure that they are not only configured but in full running order so that from the first minute your salespeople can be trained. There will be a guarantee in this way of absolutely no error on the day. On condition we get a signed agreement now'. The deal was agreed.

Way 36 Don't give goodwill concessions

Many trainers use the term 'goodwill concession' to describe one-way movement on your part for which you have not asked for any return. Why do unskilled negotiators wrongly do this? Such concessions are often given incorrectly to get the negotiation concluded, or even to start it in the first place. The reality is that it makes your counterpart stronger.

These concessions are often given out of insecurity or discomfort, usually because of lack of knowledge about what to do. That's why it is so important to develop our negotiating skills. This is most typical with the business owner who does not enjoy selling, marketing or negotiation. He has made a proposal, calculated the price, the other person seems reasonable and appears to have a need for the service but the final agreement seems stuck. Out of simple *naiveté* or often out of frustration, the business owner will give a concession out of purported goodwill.

This is wrong and seriously so. First, the other person will take advantage of the concession and invariably ask for more. Second, the profit level of the job is now eroded and will affect the owner, his staff, perhaps even his company's viability. Third, it will affect his motivation for this job, for this client. It will leave a sour taste that need not have been there. The hard fact is, it was his lack of competence and no fault of the other party. The more damaging, long-term impact is the erosion of confidence in his own business skills — all so easily rectified.

These one-way movements are sometimes given 'to get the deal moving'. Of course movement is essential but it must always be two-way. A good phrase to handle this situation is, 'If you . . . then we will . . . '. These four words are the nearest we will get to a magic phrase, because they force us to trade and not to give. They always facilitate a response.

One-way movement like this creates a precedent which will rear its head every subsequent time you negotiate with the same person. They will expect it from you, you will be weakened by the historic fact and the current pressure it is placing you under.

Rules for Making Concessions

Way 37 Trade in small steps

Be stingy. When we offer something, make the other person work for it. Trade concessions reluctantly one by one. It makes buyers think they have got to our bottom line. We need to avoid making larger concessions as the negotiation progresses, in fact each concession should be smaller than the one before.

That means of course that we have listed our concessions beforehand. We know already which ones are first on our list and we work through them one at a time. Don't indicate that there are more, otherwise you will be pressed for more.

Way 38 Trade concessions one at a time

We live an age of time pressure. Often negotiations are damaged because we rush in and give away too soon and too much. With busy managers, owners, partners, there is a tendency to give away a large concession, to speed up and conclude the negotiation process. You may even be thinking, 'This negotiation is not really worth this much time, there is so much else to do'.

A better way of viewing the same situation is to calculate how much time has already gone into this negotiation: your technical people, your presentation, your revisions and not least the amount of time you have already put in. All this is at risk because the pressure of time is urging you to come up with a solution now. There may even be an issue of personal confidence here. You may want a quick and apparently successful outcome to boost your own confidence. Resist it. Remember your predetermined commitment, bite your tongue and trade concessions one by one — slowly.

You might say, 'I need to reflect, I need to talk to . . . '. What we think of our skill depends on how the bargaining goes. When we reach agreement too quickly, we later think we are a lousy negotiator.

Remember how we saw earlier, 'Never say Yes first time'. This applies to the trading of concessions. When either buyer or seller reach agreement too quickly, they will wonder if they made a mistake or not. When you feel under any pressure to say 'Yes', say 'No' and buy some time.

Way 39 Aim higher than you think

I give you this heading slightly 'tongue in cheek'. But the truth is that most people worry about how *low* they should start, rather than how *high* they should aim. 'Aim higher and you will come out better', all the trainers say that. 'How much higher is the age-old question'. 'Test it' is the answer. You will never know if you could get more until you have asked for more.

People often ask me, 'How much should I charge for my time, my product, my service?' There are some simple tests you can run, to check the impact of price. You compare with other similar offerings in your market, you ask yourself about your own confidence in your pricing levels. Ask yourself if there is some way in which you can package your product or service to make it appear in a different league.

You can test with direct mail. Send out an offer with tests on, say, four different prices. Monitor the response and see what percentage return you get with each test price. You may find that all four yield the same return. That would indicate that there is still more room for price movement. You may find that price 4 — the highest — yields just half the response of price 2, which is exactly half the price. Then you have a value judgement: Do I want fewer customers at the higher price — maybe less invoicing, less administration? Or do I want more customers at a lower price because I have other things I can sell them?

Make sure you have a clear rationale for the price you ask. And communicate it with strength and conviction. Here again the USP will work for you. The stronger it is, the more measurable its effect, the better your chances for higher pricing. At least by aiming high you give yourself maximum room to negotiate.

If a buyer presses you on price, it may be because he is not convinced that your service is worth what you are asking. That means that your USP is not clear, not relevant or miscommunicated. Alternatively, if they think your services are very valuable they may be willing to pay a great deal more for it than they tell you.

If you are in buying mode it often works well to ask for a shocking discount, well over what any reasonable person would expect. Give yourself room. Whether we are buying or selling, remember it is very difficult to trade up. If we aim higher than we think it is very easy to trade down.

Way 40 Don't split the difference

Of all the tactics in negotiation, this one is probably the most commonly used. Even the most inexperienced person will resort to this tactic. Why? Because it resolves a potential sticking point and brings the agreement nearer in what appears to be a 'fair' manner. It is an apparently easy way out for the inexperienced negotiator and provides a face saving way out for both parties.

Don't split the difference. Let's say we are buying. We want to buy at £80,000 and our seller wants £90,000. He may well say, 'Let's split the difference'. Don't settle for £85,000. If the other person uses the phrase, 'Let's split the difference', our answer will be, 'We couldn't afford to do that, but I'll tell you what we could do. If you will . . . then we will . . . '.

This tactic is commonly applied by both buyer and seller. It is attractive because it brings the end in sight. We can often succumb because of the apparently reachable agreement. If we respond and simply split the difference then we will lose money. We should trade a concession and without doubt improve our deal. Price is usually the last thing we want to trade so we must have other things ready to trade first.

As a buyer even if you ultimately had to shift on price, you will end up moving to £82,000 and not £85,000. That one skill alone has just saved your company £3000.

One of my clients was negotiating a large sale where the customer was obliged to pay up-front for a 12-month supply. The customer was very concerned about paying up-front for 12 months and was more than a little nervous about the credibility of the company. He asked for two month's trial supply. This is never acceptable, simply because the service takes six months usage before results show positively. My client thought to himself, 'I will meet him halfway' and offered a six-month trial on condition that signed agreement was reached that day. Both of them accepted and to be honest both were wrong. They had effectively split the difference. What he should have done is to ask for more, he had given too much too soon. The buyer responded wrongly in accepting the split difference, he should have responded, 'I can't do that, but what I can is . . .'.

Way 41 Watch out for the shocker

I shall never forget the moment. My wife and I were buying a house. It was advertised on the market for £230,000 and my wife suggested, 'Why don't you shock them with an offer of £140,000. In fact,' she said,' if I phone them and offer £135,000, will you give me the saved £5000 for the garden?' I assented and she made the call. They were duly shocked. But we settled to my amazement at £135,000!

Why did we do that? There was nothing to lose. If we had been unsuccessful we could still have come back with a sensible offer nearer their original asking figure. Using a shocking opening position can really unsettle an inexperienced opponent.

When someone tries it on you be prepared. If you are ready for it you won't get angry and walk out!

Say, 'Thank you for your offer. As you can imagine this is not even close. I will leave this for now and ask if you would kindly reflect on it. Maybe I can come back to you to see if it would be possible to find a way forward'.

We have kept the relationship intact. We have given him a face-saving way back into the negotiation, but we have defended our price. Often in response he will laugh and say, 'Just checking, now what would be close?' That is a very good ploy if you are buying because it now gently coerces the seller to state a view on price which has hopefully been leveraged downwards.

If you are selling you might say, 'I would like to come back to that in just a moment, what I would like to do first is to run through an outline of the whole proposed deal'.

Way 42 Don't be first to accede to pressure on primary items

Never be the first to concede on primary items. Always begin on secondary items. We know from our analysis which concessions are primary and which secondary. Try to ensure that your counterpart is the first to yield on a primary point. Remember that this negotiation will end at some position between your ideal and his. The closer to your ideal you can get, the better off you are. If you make the first primary concession, the chances are that the negotiation will swing more in your opponent's favour, simply because we have given something too large or too valuable too soon.

We are endeavouring all the time to 'match and trade'. That is why it is so important to trade carefully. If you feel that you are getting close to exhausting your secondary options, ask him for something primary in return for a secondary move of your own. But never match a primary concession of your own for a secondary one of his.

This gets particularly acute as a deadline nears. Be particularly watchful when deadlines of any sort are involved. You may well find yourself ensnared by a deadline which you imposed earlier in the negotiation process. You can buy yourself time by suggesting you call your office to see if there is any way that deadline could be extended by minutes, hours or even days.

Way 43 Help the other person to feel he has a good deal

When we finish the negotiation and come to agreement, it is very important to the fulfilment of the agreement reached, and the long-term relationship involved that we don't gloat over any apparent victory. Remembering our maxim of Win

Win, we should be at pains to help the other party feel that they have a good deal.

If you were buying, and your seller feels one or more of the following, he will feel positive about the outcome, he will feel he has a bargain:

- If he feels he has done better than his competitors

- If the price is good for him in terms of profit, volume delivery etc

- If he is confident in your prompt payment and supplier loyalty

- If he has extracted some form of 'guarantee' from you

- If he feels there is a genuinely good chance of future business.

Whether you are the buyer or seller, tell the other person that he is a real professional. Build his respect and affirmation. It will also build his appreciation and respect for you.

If you were selling why not write to or fax your buyer, congratulate him on the terms he has secured. Affirm in writing some of the key points that he has negotiated and affirm your commitment to service and customer care. Talk about your pleasure at welcoming him as a customer and build in positive comments about the anticipated long-term relationship. Why not even send some personalised and appropriate greeting card. Helping the counterpart to feel good can be as simple as giving him unexpectedly 'one more than he expected'. One more can be one more anything.

I was speaking in the USA recently. A building contractor in Miami was telling me how after he finishes every job — when the snagging terms have been negotiated and agreed — he always gives one more thing. What he usually does is to landscape some small, area or plant some special trees — free — as his way of saying thank you. He has been doing that for 18 years and has kept many of his clients for the whole of that time. They obviously felt they got a good deal.

Way 44 Maximise the value of what you offer

Raise the value of what we are offering. We do this by raising the apparent cost to us, using phrases like 'That would create a precedent' or 'That would be very difficult'. If there is no apparent or believable cost to us, we are really conceding or trading nothing in the mind of our opponent.

The more we can maximise the value of what we have to offer, then the greater the concession appears to be. Here is a simple checklist to help establish the value of any concession we make:

- Imply that it is very difficult to give, for example because of your superior technology, the technicalities of the process involved or the cost involved etc

- Where it helps your case, quantify that cost, and multiply it up, for example the cost per annum, the cost if every buyer or user had the same arrangement. Doing this you can quite easily make it appear totally unreasonable and in doing so lower his aspiration

- Refer to major problems solved, or obstacles removed

- Refer to savings gained and quantify wherever possible

- Refer to past gains either for this company or for other companies which you can use as testimonial material

- Imply that this is not your company policy

- Refer to opportunities that it can open up

- Refer to preferences it can satisfy.

Way 45 Minimise the value of what he is offering

Lower the value of what he is offering. Reduce the cost to him. 'Surely you would incur that cost anyway?' Reduce the apparent value to us, 'That's of no real value to us', or 'That's of little value to us'. Reduce his aspirations, his concessions need to appear meaningless.

Here is a simple checklist to help reduce the impact of what he is offering us by way of concession:

- Treat it as if it is no real concession. Make him feel that it is like vapourware.

- Suggest that it is only what is expected in cases like these.

- Suggest that they would incur those costs anyway — implying no extra cost.

- Suggest that other companies you deal with, always give and often give more.

- Suggest that you have the potential benefits of this concession already.

Way 46 Do it aloud, don't just think it!

At the end of this trading phase, always summarise the details. Restate all the points of agreement and summarise what they contain. Write them down and let the other person see what you have written. Turn the paper round so that it is facing him. But make sure that you voice it all — speak it out. This applies to maximising or minimising the effect of concessions. Don't just think about how valuable your concession is. Don't just think about how insignificant his response is, say it, and say it clearly.

Look for Negotiable Variables

We must stop seeing price as the key issue. The most common mistake made by inexperienced negotiators is a default preoccupation with price. We must learn a change of mindset where we don't think price and where we do think negotiable variable. In other words, our minds need to be full of all the variables surrounding each potential deal. Best of all are the ones cheap to us and valuable to the buyer.

Way 47 Find areas for negotiable variables

We have seen their importance but now we have to come up with some. How do we go about determining where our negotiable variables lie? How do we determine them and evaluate their relative worth? The checklist below is a helpful starting-point:

- The product or service itself — ask yourself: How could it be changed, what elements can be added or removed? What are the implications to the other party in terms of cost, longevity, quality etc?

- What specific functions or attributes does it have — do they vary with different applications or in different markets?

- The impact of promotion or publicity that surrounds it.

- Expenditure. Think through implications of the manner of payment. Credit terms or direct debits. Discounts. Progress payments and prepayments.

- Volume. Think through implications of packaging, storage, insurance. Who pays for what?

- Quality. What does quality mean and to whom? Can you substantiate cost additions or reductions for varying levels of quality? Can you quantify what variations mean to your counterpart — what they might be worth to him?

- Delivery arrangements (amounts, locations, frequency).

- Maintenance, service or aftersales care.

- Guarantees or warranties.

Way 48 Identify key variables and their place in the negotiation

Having located the general area of where we can find these concessions or tradeable variables we must now home in and identify more accurately how we can use them.

Seven key questions emerge here:

1. What concessions do we normally make?

2. What is their value to our counterpart? Have we quantified that value in measurable terms?

3. What would we like to have in return?

4. What other tradeables do we have? (Refer to Way 47.)

5. What could we concede that costs us little but has high value to our counterpart?

6. What can he reciprocate that may be low cost to him but valuable to us?

7. What negotiable variables could we build into our offer/proposal in the first place?

From these prompts, make sure that you have taken the time to list all your tradeables, your negotiable variables. You should have a typed list of up to 20 of them. You should know how much they cost per month, or per year. You should know the impact on your cost or profit of each of these concessions — even multiplied by the number of customers that you have. You should have a clear idea of their value to your counterpart.

Way 49 Build in some negotiable variables

When you have exhausted your list of current actual trade-ables, ask yourself what other negotiable variables you could build in that you don't yet have. The answer lies in discovering what you could add to your product, service or offering, perhaps bundling it into a package and then peeling off certain non-essential layers as tradeable concessions.

Alternatively you evaluate the tradeables and, if they are fairly low cost to you, add them as concessions which you can trade, in return for something else from your counterpart.

My main business is in training and consultancy and I regularly conduct strategic marketing reviews for small to medium sized companies. What I have done is to build in some negotiable variables. One of them is a helpline which gives qualified telephone back-up support to the implementation process of the plan produced.

Another variable is a health check at six-monthly intervals. I can build them into the original offer and then use them to trade. Or I can leave them out of the original offer and add them at the trading phase.

When I am buying, I am busy thinking about what negotiable variables I can conjure up for my potential suppliers. A good example of this comes from running seminars.

Most hotels have a so called fixed rate — full day only — for seminar rooms. I always ask them, 'What is your price for a full day?' They might say, '£800'. I say, 'I want it for a half day only, I will be cleared out by 12 noon, I would like to book it for £ 350'. They usually splutter and mutter but I very rarely have to pay the full day rate even though that is printed policy.

I then turn to the tea and biscuits. I ask,'How much for tea and biscuits?' They say, '£1.90 per person'. I say, 'I am running upwards of 100 seminars per year, most of your competitors will do just tea for £1 — can you better that please?' A bit of trading then ensues, but I will not pay for the biscuits. That trading alone will save me or my sponsoring clients £5000 or more per annum. Do that for 10 years and it has saved £50,000. I point out that fact to any reluctant conference manager and they are usually a little shocked. I don't think I have ever been refused.

Way 50 Determine whether the negotiation is long term or short term

A hunter goes out to get enough for the one meal, farming looks for a long-term ongoing supply. The rules are very different. If this negotiation is definitely a one-off deal you can afford to be a hunter — more demanding, more insistent and more intent on your interests. Stalk your prey, make your kill and devour the proceeds.

In the main, however, we have to deal with the same people, the same companies over and over. It is much closer to farming. Farming is long term, looking for a return each year or each season. That means the deals we secure have to sustain a relationship over an extended period. In the process, we have to uncover negotiable variables that make sense for the other person in the long term as well as the short. Remember, we have to live out the consequences of our negotiation.

Potential Sources of Negotiable Variables

Looking more specifically at some of these sources of tradeables will help us to focus our aim and be more precise. These tradeables are not just good in the sense that they help us to achieve the agreement both parties are seeking, but they are doubly helpful in that they also produce long-term deals that stick. If both parties are motivated by the agreement, we are doubly successful.

Way 51 Payment

There is so much scope for negotiation on terms — particularly in the UK where there is considerable government lobbying on this very issue. Even our old friend the tax office is open to some honest negotiation when it comes to repaying overdue tax.

In eight years running this particular business I have never had one bad debt. How is that? Very simply I always ask for a cheque on the day, with every new client, and a cheque on the last day of the month for every long-term client. No one has ever queried paying on the day. It has the advantage of being related close in time to the services rendered. In other words, in my field — seminars — people are usually highly motivated at the end of the seminar and it is not painful for them to part with the money. One month or two months later a lot of that feel-good factor will have been dissipated by the normal daily grind.

Why not say, *'If you can* give us a cheque on the day rather than your 60-day terms, *we can* provide a further half day of helpline time'. Consultants, and professionals like accountants, why not negotiate your payment on direct debit and say, '*If we can agree* monthly direct debit starting this month *then we can reduce* the annual fee by £800'.

Buyers use payment terms creatively. Very few sellers do. You can actually motivate them to trade concessions by the simplest of adjustments to payment.

Caution: Do not ever accept normal practice as binding. As long as it is ethical there is no reason whatever for you to be bound by years of so called 'normal' — in reality damaging — practice.

Way 52 Quantity

Think through the implications of volume on your buying or selling. If it is a product perhaps you say, '*I can lower the price from X if you take Y*'. If you are a consultant say, '*We can* provide the research for £1000 per annum each office, rather than £1200 *if you* include your regional offices'.

If you are the buyer, think creatively about how you can use volume to your advantage. You might say, 'How important is volume to you, at what point does increased volume impact your production — positively or negatively?' This can apply to the purchase of fixed price items that have become virtual commodities.

I was recently buying a Pentium P5–100 PC for my office. At least my son Josh assures me that it really is for my office. I knew from previous experience that asking for a discount did not work, but I talked about volume and discovered that if you bought 12 you could get one free. It then became an option for me to act as a co-ordinator for some of my friends and acquaintances in buying bulk.

Way 53 Time

There are all kinds of factors which can be considered. Think of the timing of delivery, further shipments, progress reports. Closing dates, deadlines. Think through the time related elements of your own sale or purchase and use those elements to advantage.

A number of my clients run subscription based services, where the contract is an annual membership fee. It is quite costly to renew these customers each year and there are some genuine savings if a customer will agree to a two or three-year contract. It makes sense to offer something for those extended agreements when necessary.

Another variation is offered by the Marketing Guild which has a nominal annual membership fee payable by direct debit on a 'till forbid' basis. In the unlikely event that a member wants to cease membership, they offer a no quibble refund, proportional to the unexpired period of that subscription.

A useful way to probe for a concession is to say, 'We will accept your figure if you will make it a three-year contract instead'. Or, 'We will agree your figure if you agree to a six-monthly implementation review'.

When you are in buying mode, think through some variables which you could use beneficially. If you know you need the product or service for three or more years why not suggest, 'We could pay you what you are asking but not quite yet. What we could do is pay 90 per cent of your asking price this year, 95 per cent next year and your current quoted price in year three. If that was acceptable we could sign a three-year contract subject to conditions'.

Way 54 More or less?

An obvious way to trade is to add or remove items from the agreement. It may work for you to have more, it may work for him to have less.

The art is to think these through before the negotiation starts so that you are crystal clear about the cost or profit implications. For example, 'If you will agree to a quarterly review we can reduce the audit fee by 10 per cent. If you let us supply all your TV's both for sale and rental we will add Ceefax to each unit'.

Creative buying instincts can quickly find a use for these tradeables. 'If you can agree this price adjustment on our corporate brochure, we will commit ourselves to take 500 A4 flyers at your list price.' This works even better if you knew from the beginning that the 500 flyers have to be bought from somewhere. Doing your homework here will pay dividends.

There are all kinds of options open to us if we will think creatively about the specification of our requirement or our product/service. One way to test is to say, '*If we can eliminate* this area then *we can accept* your proposal of £10,000. *If we can reduce* the desk research *then we can adjust* the price'.

You say, 'You can have the manuals, if we can have two months to write your plan rather than three weeks'. If he says 'No, we certainly can't do that', you have discovered that time is a key issue. That information then tells you what is highly valuable to him and often what is low cost to you. You can then trade more intelligently.

Way 55 A strategy for referrals

In our training we encourage clients to adopt a simple strategy for referrals by asking their customers for referrals routinely, every three months. A marvellous technique is to build it in as a negotiable. This should be high on our list of favourites because it costs nothing and yet has a very high real and perceived value. If you are selling why not use it like this, '*I'll agree* to the price you want, *if you arrange* a presentation with . . . '? Could be another branch, another division or a colleague in another company with a similar usage or requirement. Or 'We will agree to this very special pricing structure, if you will invite ten other potential users to your factory, and act as a positive reference site. We will also feel free to bring prospective clients of our own to the site at mutually agreed frequencies and at arranged times'.

One of my friends developed a marvellous sales tracking software, with macros for sales letters, recalls and networked fax applications. His company negotiated to develop it for a local company at cost. They did this simply because they wanted a multi-user reference site which had networked fax application. They ultimately invited a number of prospects to the site including an international distributor. The distributor was so impressed that they incorporated the software into their suite of programmes and their national distribution programme.

Way 56 The magic 'if'

Did you notice all the words emphasised in italics from Ways 51–55? Let me highlight them for you:

'I can . . . if you take'

'We can . . . if you'

'We will accept . . . if you will make'

'We will agree . . . if you agree'

'If you can . . . we can'

'If you will . . . we can'

'If you let us supply . . . we will add'

'If you can agree . . . we will commit'

'If we can agree . . . then we can reduce'

'I'll agree . . . if you arrange'

'If we can eliminate . . . we can accept . . .'

'If we can reduce . . . then we can adjust'

You spotted the 'magic' word — *if*. It is in every sentence that forms part of our trading phase. We use 'If' every time we make a proposal. It makes it clear that movement is expected and puts gentle pressure on that movement.

If tells him the price of your revised offer, or the price of your movement. If he wants something from you it will cost him and the 'magic *If*' makes that very clear.

Way 57 Use silence

It is quite all right to have silence, you are not obliged to talk. The fact is, the one who talks more, gives more away. The more you talk, the more information you are likely to be giving the other person. That information increases his authority in the negotiation — every time!

If you get thrown at any time — and it happens to the most experienced — give yourself time to think. Ask to use the phone, take a toilet break. Tell them you need a bit of fresh air and ask for 15 minutes. Or just sit in silence doodling or writing on your paper. If they get embarrassed, don't let it worry you, tell them what is going on and say, 'Excuse me while I think this through for a few moments', or ' Excuse me I just need a few moments of silence while I calculate the impact of this for both of us'. If you are negotiating on the telephone, silence is a useful ploy. The other party feels compelled to break it.

Equally, when the deal is agreed don't hang around. Many a good deal has been badly damaged by the talking that ensued. Many of you will find a propensity to verbal diarrhoea at this point. The reason is, there has been so much control, so much pent up energy. But if you lose the deal here you can lose it in a big way.

I remember negotiating one deal for a client. I had an experienced technical person with me. He knew his role and he was brilliant, he let me lead. He only contributed when I drew him in. But I forgot to tell him Way 57. As soon as the deal was struck he thought the rules had changed. He began discussing at length how he would overcome certain technical problems. Those problems had not even surfaced during the negotiation. Weeks of work, and thousands of pounds were blown with just a few minutes' careless words.

Handling Deadlock

It is one of the most counterproductive and undesirable of all the conclusions in a negotiation. We should be alert for its possibilities and try to avoid it. The only exception is where we threaten deadlock as a tactic to galvanise our counterpart into action. The main cause of deadlock is the absence of sufficient negotiable variables being used. The more variables you can arm yourself with at the start the less likely it is that you will be deadlocked.

Way 58 Watch out for frustration

Reaching a deadlock is a frustrating experience. Usually a lot of time has gone into it. You may have already made one or two visits, your proposals have been put together with hours of work and now you have deadlock. One of the biggest dangers is that you will react badly out of frustration, particularly if this is a large deal and you are getting tired. We can see this illustrated often, when trade unions and employers have long, arduous negotiating sessions, day and night. When there is deadlock it produces a certain type of aggression which causes one or both parties to make unwise statements or unwise moves.

Be aware of it, be prepared for it and be careful how you act when in the middle of it.

Way 59 Avoid immovable positions

We can get to the situation where neither of you feel you can budge. At this point a new dynamic occurs, in the sense that you are now opponents rather than counterparts. If you dig in and declare a firm unalterable position, it is more than likely that they will too. Immovable positions should be avoided to prevent deadlock.

The builder had quoted a fixed price for a loft conversion. One particular aspect was the staircase. The local building regulation department proved unusually fussy and insisted on some specific changes to the staircase as the drawing specification was unacceptable. Extra charges were incurred, not just on the revised staircase itself, but on all the fittings required. Deadlock was imminent. In a case like this, if you are belligerent the customer will invariably put his foot down and insist that the builder absorb all the costs. The builder would equally expect the customer to pay all. Immovable positions are taken and deadlock looms.

A better way is to review the whole project positively with him. It's his home, his project. Ask the client his opinion, what he likes and dislikes. Ask him if he would be willing to pay a little extra for something that would end up significantly better. Is he willing to enhance the whole ship for a 'halfpennyworth of tar'? Exploring a whole variety of options can save the day when he would otherwise have dug in his heels.

The builder in this case should have the ideal in his mind and have a minimum acceptable figure as his bottom line.

Way 60 Avoid price rot

Sometimes, however, and more commonly in business negotiations, the buyer threatens deadlock to panic the seller into price rot. This is a dreadful disease — painful and sometimes terminal. The buyer threatens seller with a phrase like, 'Unless we can agree to this price reduction, I see no way forward'.

The buyer can succumb to the threat, and in doing so rot his price structure for ever. He can dig his own heels in, declare an immovable position, and counter threat. That is not always wrong, it can call his counterpart's bluff. Most appropriately he can defend his price but trade concessions.

The moral is simple, don't allow the threat of deadlock to panic you into price rot as a seller, or a price hike if you are the buyer.

Way 61 The bridging moment

We can do ourselves and the long-term relationship a great deal of good if we can take control calmly, but in a manner which has clearly got both parties' best interests at heart.

We achieve that by moving into the bridging moment, and we handle the deadlock with a phrase like this, 'Mr Counterpart, we have both put a lot of effort into this, let us have one more go before we admit defeat'. Or, 'There is real value in the time and effort that have gone in from both sides, could we look at this one more time?' And then begin asking W questions again, open ended questions.

Alternatively, we can use the bridging moment to agree positively on what we have determined. Use Way 57 to buy a little bit of time, then summarise where you feel the negotiation has moved forward positively. Write down the key points in summary form. Then use a bridging phrase like this, 'It seems we are both pleased with the points of agreement we have covered, but clearly we have an area here where there seems to be no possibility of progress today. Can I suggest that we agree another meeting say in one week, when we have both had time to reflect creatively. How does that sound?'

Or you might suggest, 'It may help both of us if we break here and work informally on heads of agreement, and come back together informally next week. How does that sound?' Emphasising the informal context is often enough to get the process moving again. It takes the intensity out of the moment, gives time for reflection, and enables both parties to save face.

Way 62 Make a statement, ask a question

Whether you are making one more attempt now to break the deadlock, or are meeting informally later, this key skill will enable you to move the process forward. It is an accepted fact that whoever is asking questions is in control. Being in control is your responsibility. If you want to be effective in your negotiation, the only way you can maintain that control at this point is by making an acceptable statement and then following it with a series of W questions.

W questions are absolutely vital, simply because they are your only chance of getting the buyer talking again. For example, 'We are going to come back again informally. Could I ask, what do you feel most strongly about? What in your opinion could change our problem? How would you feel about a 24-month option? What is it that you do like about our proposal?' You may well find in some cases that this technique enables you fairly easily and naturally to go back to negotiating again.

Whether it does or doesn't, the W questions will give you information that can enhance the process of reflection which will now have to take place.

Way 63 The way forward

There are only three productive outcomes possible. Either we have one more attempt at negotiation there and then, or we meet later at an agreed time to discuss our reflected views informally. Or we meet again in a more formal setting.

Whichever of the three is chosen it is vital that you keep positive, and communicate in a positive manner. Before you part, make sure you have documented a brief summary of agreement so far. You may well be able to document the particular issues that you will need to reflect on or report on informally. Where you have asked W questions you may want to jot down the key concerns that you have uncovered. If your counterpart has uncovered concerns of yours, jot them down as well. Reaffirm your commitment to work for a solution. Reaffirm your desire to do business with your counterpart. Thank him for his effort and energy. Way 65 details specific techniques for asking questions.

When you get back to the office, type up your summary notes and fax or mail them to him. Make sure that you repeat your commitment to arriving at a mutually beneficial agreement.

One alternative, as a last resort, would be to jointly agree for two other negotiators to have an informal chat. It could be your managing directors or your technical directors. The latter is risky, and you would have to ensure that they were reasonably competent and also that they were thoroughly briefed.

Asking Questions

Way 64 Asking questions is the method of navigation

The primary key to staying in control is to ask questions. Whoever is asking questions is by inference leading, directing, shaping. If at any moment in any phase you feel that control is slipping from your grasp, then make a statement, ask a question, and you are easily back in control. Asking questions is the only way you can find out what other than price is really important to this individual or company. In a free market economy there are only two pivotal points around which a deal is ultimately agreed:

1. Price

2. The benefit, advantage or gain, that your counterpart could experience as a result of agreeing the terms.

Asking appropriate questions is the only way in which you can uncover what your counterpart feels, needs or wants in the area of benefit, advantage or gain. Putting it another way, the questions you ask and the resultant answers demonstrate the criteria by which your counterpart will evaluate your proposal or bargaining process.

Asking intelligent questions implies that you will have competent solutions or answers. Asking questions is the only way that you can express interest in your counterpart's goals, needs, objectives and aspirations. Asking questions will give you information that others do not have, information that will build your authority and give you the edge.

Way 65 Use open-ended questions

If questioning is so vital, what kind of questions should we be asking? We should be asking open-ended questions. Closed questions are questions to which the only answer is 'Yes' or 'No'. They produce no additional information, they close down the conversation, they close down the proper negotiation process too early. Typical closed questions are prefaced with; Do you?, Could you?, Will you?

Open-ended questions cannot be answered 'Yes' or 'No'; they always produce a response and always yield information. In training circles they are loosely referred to as W questions. They include, What?, Which?, When?, Why?, Who? and the odd one out: How? They always generate information and they are key to retaining control at every stage of the negotiation process.

A builder had negotiated a deal with a Baptist church for renovation work valued at £120,000. The deal appeared to be agreed, but the architect simply would not give the builder the start date. The builder was stalled for some weeks and could not get a clear picture from the architect. In a move to get things under way the managing director of the building company approached the church direct and began asking W questions to attempt to discover the nature of the problem. It transpired that the church wanted to carry on meeting in the building while the renovations were going on. They had been told that it would not be possible. The builder simply offered to find alternative accommodation while the work was in hand — offering to pay for it himself. The cost of that was a few hundred pounds but would have the effect of releasing £120,000 of work.

Subsequently with the goodwill his gesture generated, he was able to develop a method of working which enabled the church to carry on meeting — with some temporary facilities — but within their existing premises. The job is now under way.

The Authority of your Counterpart

Way 66 Ensure your counterpart has the authority to negotiate

Negotiation can only succeed between equals who both have the authority to agree on any of the decisions that will need to be reached. If either party — buyer or seller — do not have that authority, the negotiation cannot be concluded. It is important to understand what authority levels exist in your counterpart's company.

Part of the necessary questioning process is to establish the real authority of your counterpart and any team members he may introduce. As a general observation it should be obvious that both parties must have the authority and the determination to change the various components of an agreement. In other words, it is no value getting to the bargaining phase, only to find out that your counterpart does not have the authority to agree on the tradeable variables.

The first question is, what title does my counterpart have? Does that title clearly establish his authority? Even if he is senior partner or managing director you can check by asking the innocent question, 'Who else is involved in the decision-making process?'

Where his title is less clear we must check if he has the authority that the negotiation requires. State, 'We are going to move to the final negotiation phase next Tuesday, can I take it that you have the authority to agree the final terms?' or, 'Who else in your organisation needs to be involved in agreeing the final terms?' If there is anyone else, make sure that they are there.

Way 67 Check the power behind the scenes

Often there are influencers and powerful contributors who are behind the scenes. By using W questions we must uncover:

- What other individuals are consulted before decisions are reached?

- Whose opinions help to set strategy, tactics and policy for our counterpart?

- Does the decision require an expert or technical specialist's approval?

- Who are those experts, and what is the extent of their influence?

Way 68 Manage the power behind the scenes

During the preparation phase we should have uncovered the existence of these individuals and either found a way to negotiate them out of the process or, more likely, insisted that we meet them at an early stage so that we can build our knowledge of the factors important to each one.

We then ask for an informal meeting with all of them present. We have met or telephoned each one individually beforehand. We make an informal presentation which takes into account all their individual requirements. During this informal presentation we ask each one in turn if all their requirements have been satisfied. When we are clear that they have, we either move into negotiation, or agree to reconvene with our counterpart, to conduct the negotiation proper.

Tough or Effective?

Way 69 Characteristics of the effective negotiator

Being tough is not the same as being effective. Often, being tough leads to immovable positions which create negative feelings and more frequently lead to negotiations that are deadlocked. The source of the toughness usually lies in incompetence or insecurity. Applying some of these 101 ways will build your competence.

The effective negotiator will have the following attributes:

- Knows his ideal and works patiently and consistently for it
- Can be tough if and only if that would be productive
- Is very slow and rather mean in giving concessions
- Is not frightened by the thought of deadlock
- Never makes it seem he has 'won' a point
- Always prepares his information and thinks through the possible obstacles
- Always rehearses the approach.

Way 70 The effective negotiator looks at buying and selling in the same deal

One of my colleagues sells PCs and software. They recently negotiated the biggest deal ever in their 14-year history. The contract was to supply PCs and services across Europe. First they looked for a way to earn authority by choosing to take on a small deal worth just a few thousand pounds. They saw the potential not in the job but in the customer. Price was stated to be a key issue so they enhanced their credibility by going back through the supply chain. The customer wanted extra discount; my colleague insisted that for an increased discount of 1.5 per cent the order should be increased from 45 to 70 units. The discount didn't cost him, it actually gained him more profit on the whole deal. Because of the discount the customer then discovered some unused end of year budget and placed a further £100,000.

My colleague asked for payment on delivery and got it! In turn they negotiated 60 days payment terms from their supplier. They now had the additional benefit of several hundred thousand pounds earning interest for 60 days.

In the purchasing process they went first to distributors and evaluated the distributors on the basis of a similar quote for 40 machines. They tested on interest shown, speed of response and hunger.

Having decided which distributor they preferred, they then went direct to the manufacturer and negotiated a few extra percentage points. They discussed other ways in which they could improve their margins. The end result was a pleased customer, a happy distributor, a willing and co-operative manufacturer and a much richer colleague. They looked at both sides of the negotiating equation.

Way 71 The effective negotiator balances his team carefully

There may well be occasional or more frequent times when the negotiation requires more than one person on your team. It may be superiors. It may be technical experts. Whoever is involved there must be clear ground rules:

- You are responsible.

- That means you have the authority on the day. Your MD or manager must make that clear and be there in a supporting role.

- Other team members know that they defer to you. You have set clear parameters of what they can and cannot say, and when they can say it.

- They know that they only contribute when drawn in by you.

- You summarise at every stage of agreement.

- You agree the final deal — after which they shut up!

If you are wise you will have rehearsed the possible outcomes with your team. Let them know where their danger points occur. Your counterpart should not have more people than you, nor should he have experts present in fields that you do not.

Way 72 The effective negotiator keeps the whole package in mind

Above all, the effective negotiator has trained himself to avoid the ever open trap of price preoccupation. He keeps the whole proposal in mind all the time, and keeps it in his counterpart's thinking all the time as well.

The whole package includes:

- The product or service itself
- Particular functions or attributes
- The benefits of those functions or attributes
- The overall benefit or gain of using or investing in the service
- The positive or negative impact of publicity surrounding his company or product range
- Quantity
- Delivery
- Payment options
- Clearance of existing stocks
- Maintenance and service
- Price and profit.

Price is last, because in his mind it is just one of many potential ingredients and not the pivotal point of the agreement. In the process of keeping the whole deal in mind he will ask for all concerns and all objections when any single point is raised. He will then say, 'Can I now take it that those represent all your concerns?'

One of my associates was trying to negotiate an increase in his daily fee of 5 per cent from a long-term client who had been using our staff for nearly three years (one day per week). The client was important to him and was understandably reluctant to pay more.

My colleague thought through the whole package and came up with a solution that delighted the client, but gave him not 5 per cent but around 20 per cent! How did he do it? He reduced his daily fee by £30, and asked in return for £75 commission for every tender enquiry generated. My colleague was totally safe, knowing he would average more than one tender enquiry per day worked, thus yielding him an average increase of 20 per cent. The client was delighted because the fee was now performance related. All that, simply by keeping the whole deal in mind.

Way 73 The effective negotiator has a good alternative

If you have no alternative to this particular negotiated agreement, you are weakened and constrained. The effective negotiator understands this clearly and endeavours to have a good fallback position.

Fallback in this sense means the best alternative course of action open to you if this negotiation fails completely. It can make all the difference to where the power balance will settle. The stronger your option here, the less you will feel the need to make concessions. Equally, the more confidence you will have in making demands of the other side.

Where he has it, the effective negotiator will make sure that his counterpart understands his strength. Where he doesn't have it, he will not give that fact away!

Way 74 The effective negotiator avoids irritators

It is fairly obvious what irritators are! Things that irritate your counterpart. They would include the following:

- Unpleasant personal habits

- An over-friendly or familiar approach when the relationship is not genuinely at that level

- Bad or inappropriate language

- Smoking — never light up unless your counterpart has

- Embarrassing others who make mistakes in the negotiation process

- Voicing personal opinions about others — they nearly always backfire

- Being greedy

- Adopting a triumphant manner

- Annoying phrases — particularly ones that appear patronising or smutty.

If you don't know whether you are guilty of any of these ask a colleague whose judgement and motives you trust to point them out. An ancient proverb says 'Faithful are the wounds of a friend'. In other words, better the marginal embarrassment of a friend's observation than poor performance and potential alienation in the negotiation process.

One particular irritator is a consistent and apparently mean approach in a long-term relationship — where you keep on asking. A good example would be if you had a restaurant which you and your family like to use either regularly or from time to time. If you ask for a deal each time you go, you probably irritate some members of your family and you will irritate the proprietor because of your constant asking. It appears mean. Far better here to sit down with the proprietor and agree a long-term arrangement which leaves him motivated and gives you the deal you are looking for.

I made this mistake with my plumber. We have a fairly large home and the heating system needs urgent attention several times each year. Every time I used him he would give me excellent service — even mobile phone support out of hours — but it seemed to him that I would always haggle. In the end it irritated him and he lost the will to service me. I had made the mistake of gaining in the short term and losing out in the longer term.

Way 75 The effective negotiator embraces mistakes

One of my friends has a quotation that he wants on his tombstone, 'Where there is no ox the stall is clean, but much strength comes by the ox'. If you want the strength of the ox then we will have to put up with a bit of muck from time to time. Mistakes are the fertiliser of success. We don't much like the constituent components of fertiliser. They smell, they are unpleasant, but they do bring growth.

Mistakes in negotiation are inevitable. In this book I have deliberately quoted personal examples of where I have got it wrong. That's because it's not that abnormal. We are not omnipotent — thank God! We cannot possibly win every single situation. But when we get it wrong there is a simple choice: do we resent the experience as an intruder or welcome it as a friend?

Every mistake I have relayed in this book has taught me. Sometimes I get uptight but mostly I am grateful — it is another building block in the process of aspiring to be an effective negotiator.

Way 76 The effective negotiator has an eye for body language

I don't overrate this skill. There is so much complexity about body language that, in my experience, training in depth rarely helps because of that complexity. In other words, there is so much to learn and remember that negotiators rarely use it effectively. Nor is it a perfect science; there are different interpretations for the same body movements.

There are some simple applications, however, and the effective negotiator has learnt them. The classic ploy of some negotiators is to sit their counterpart in a chair that is lower. It can very easily make you feel less important, less confident and it is a ploy to watch out for. The same negotiator may well position your chair in a disadvantageous manner. He may have it a long way away, or at an awkward angle. Your response is simple. If you don't like the chair, simply say, 'I am uncomfortable, do you mind if I stand?' If you don't like the placement of the chair, move it with confidence and say, 'I would like to move closer if that is okay'.

Avoid sitting down in reception. You are nearly always offered low uncomfortable chairs that do not prepare you properly for the negotiation ahead. I always stand up and walk around even in the smallest of reception areas. The reason is that the receptionist cannot forget me and will do her best to get me to my appointment. I feel confident, in control, and consequently build my authority. In the process I read their brochures, look at certificates and read their in-house newsletters. I have more information.

Watch out for significant movement at critical moments in the negotiation process. I was retained by a Swedish printer to negotiate a large printing contract in the region of £1.25 million. When we were in the final stages of negotiation I went through the proposed pricing structure expecting resistance. But at that point, the buyer jumped up and in animated fashion started walking up and down. The price was in fact a very pleasant surprise, and he could hardly contain his emotion. It told me that I could have asked for more. It gave me a very strong position when it came to trading concessions.

Tightly folded arms at the start of the negotiation and again at the beginning of the bargaining phase are normal indicators of mild stress or intensity. Don't worry about them but do watch for the moment when those arms relax and slide on to the table or on to his lap. He is relaxing, and you can be increasingly confident that your requests are acceptable — there is probably a positive disposition towards your approach.

Watch out for a negative shift. Negative shifts can include 'wandering eyes' meaning that he will not look you in the face. Irritated breathing sounds, tapping fingers, leaning back over casually in the chair, an apathetic air — all these are normal signs that you have lost his interest or that he has made up his mind not to agree. You can still recover from this position with your statement-question, for example 'Something does not appear totally clear here. Can I ask, what are your feelings about the total agreement at this point?'

Way 77 The effective negotiator always stays in control

Staying in control at every stage of the negotiation is our responsibility. It is our job to get the best deal for us while helping our counterpart to feel he has a good deal himself. The only way we can do that is by staying in control.

- Set the agenda. That means you determine when the meeting takes place, where, and what the items on the agenda are.

- Type the agenda and send or fax it.

- Take control of the meeting itself. Start by going through the agenda and agreeing the process for that particular meeting.

- Lead each step of the meeting — following the six elements of negotiation.

- Summarise every point of agreement along the way.

- Summarise the final agreement.

- Put it all in writing.

If the negotiation is getting bogged down in trivial detail or if it is going off track then you must assert control. You can do this by bringing the conversation back on track with, 'I've been wondering whether . . . ?' and then move straight into the statement–question.

Way 78 Characteristics of the ineffective negotiator

The ineffective negotiator is never sure of what the right move is or isn't. He will generally not prepare and not take the process seriously.

The ineffective negotiator will show the following characteristics;

- No preparation
- No rehearsal
- No commitment to the overall objectives or the negotiation in hand
- Insecurity and uncertainty in his opening position
- He does not have or inspire confidence in his requests or proposals
- Frequently succumbs to price-rotting pressure placed on him
- Often gets bogged down in the trivial and will trivialise the important.

Dos and Don'ts

This section contains a number of practical points, easily absorbed summaries of skills or attributes that can be quickly acquired.

Way 79 Do always maintain the initiative

This is one of the golden rules. If you don't maintain the initiative you will lose three things; first, *money*. You have spent money leading up to this moment. If you throw away the initiative now the money will be wasted. Second, *control*. By applying your skills you will have generated a certain momentum, the negotiation should be moving and moving in your direction. The moment you lose the initiative you have lost that control, you will bring the negotiation to a grinding halt and both his interests and yours will be lost. The third and most damaging thing you will lose is *business*. As you well know, not all negotiations are finally concluded when we meet for the purpose. In fact in one recent survey, 50 per cent of sales negotiations were not concluded within six months. Things crop up, changes occur and we must be ready for those eventualities.

Maintaining the initiative means you predetermine the next point of contact and take responsibility for it. You will finish any conversation or any phase of the process with a closing sentence that predetermines the next point of action. 'As promised I will make a point of contacting you next Tuesday to agree our next meeting.' You make a similar statement in your confirming letter. Agree the next step if more than one meeting is likely to be necessary. You take the initiative in the first place and you don't give it back.

Way 80 Do put things in writing

Putting things in writing is so important. It helps you to keep authority and control. It avoids all kinds of embarrassing mistakes, and often helps to clarify issues that would otherwise be clouded.

Five points about writing

1. Put any agreement into writing. Wherever possible, volunteer to write the agreement or contract.

2. Write down *all key points* during the bargaining process. Be highly visible in the process. When it suits you, show them to your counterpart and agree those points together.

3. Write the agenda before you meet. If it is a group meeting we should write the agenda after we have made contact with each person, to ensure that they feel represented. Make sure you then send a copy to each individual. Remember, what is written has authority. So think through what you could carry into the negotiation with you, in the form of written statements, proposals. In many situations we can win the advantage by carrying written evidence to support our opening offer.

4. Use customer or supplier statements in typed form, to add weight to any particular point you may be making. Particularly use them to back up any claims of advantage or benefit which you may be making during the bargaining phase.

5. Written points should be on file in the event of contractual problems later.

Way 81 Do learn to use higher authority

In a negotiation it may help us if we appear to have limited authority. What we can give away is 'apparently' minimised. 'I need to discuss that with my MD' or, 'with my partner', or 'with my department manager'.

In real terms, don't go beyond your own authority. If you are reaching a point in the negotiation where you are being asked to agree terms for which you do not have the authority, use a phrase like this, 'I am authorised to negotiate within certain parameters. I can take this one back to my MD — I doubt if he will agree. But what if we could . . . '.

Do you know the boundaries of authority within which your counterpart operates? Make sure you know what he can and cannot agree. Otherwise you may trade a concession unnecessarily.

Where it helps, insist on speaking to a higher authority in your counterpart's organisation. A friend of mine was negotiating a price from his insurance company. He selected a policy from a company offering a special deal for a second car. He was refused because of a minor accident three years earlier. He would not take no for an answer. He had patiently to elevate the issue through two levels of management to find the individual to whom the gain or loss of the business really mattered, and before he finally secured his deal. The result for him was a real saving of £300 pa. The lesson learned was to escalate the process and use higher authority to get the result he wanted.

Way 82 Do conceal your emotions

Emotions — including body language — are like words: the more you express them the more give away. Try to keep a straight face which gives away nothing in particular. Avoid obvious expressions of relief, elation or panic! Anything you give away here will give clues to your counterpart.

You can of course deliberately try to use emotion or body language as a smokescreen. The problem here is that it is difficult to maintain the act, and sooner or later you are likely to be found out. The moment that happens, you will have generated some distrust. Your own standing and authority will be weakened significantly.

Way 83 Do ask for discount when paying cash

As a general rule, ask for more and you will get more. If you are paying by credit card there is always a surcharge for the person supplying you. Anything from 3 per cent to 5 per cent. Make a habit of asking for discount — say, 'I understand that the credit card costs you 5 per cent, if I pay by cash, I assume that I can knock that off the bill'.

It won't work all the time because there are some people who actually prefer the lower risk of having less cash and you will have to find another approach. But do try it anyway.

Way 84 Do use experts

There are times when it can be beneficial to use other people who have particular skills. If you are buying print and promotion you can read Way 96. Or you could call a company specialising in cost reduction.

I am retained from time to time to lead a team in a negotiation where the stakes are high. Or to act as the sole negotiator, where the order or supply value is high relative to other transactions which a company may make. Sometimes clients will just use me to help them prepare and rehearse. When the deal is important or valuable it makes sense to call in a professional.

It always makes sense to have everyone in a negotiation role trained. The smallest of skill improvements can make a difference of 10 per cent or more to your bottom line. I was involved in a seminar recently and the following week, three people who had put some of the material into practice were reaping rewards already after just seven days. One of them had negotiated over £50,000 of new business. One of the others had totally revised his presentation and gone in at twice the price he originally intended. The third person had always been apprehensive about the negotiating process. She discovered a new confidence and was already trying it out. There are hundreds of testimonials of individuals who have quickly saved over 10 per cent on all their buying activity.

If you regularly use hotels, there are specialists who do nothing else but negotiate special deals for customers. They charge you nothing and earn their income from the hotel paid commission. It may just save you time and give you a better deal.

Way 85 Don't expect to win them all

Negotiation can be discouraging. We can make some silly mistakes, some unnecessary comments and we lose it. Either the deal does not get concluded, or our counterpart walks away with the better deal. Often large amounts of energy, time and resource have been expended. The process can be so wearing at times.

Where you can, laugh! Reflect on something funny or absurd. Don't take it all too seriously. Ask yourself what you can learn, write it down and then apply the knowledge you have gained. Do keep enthusiastic. Business people need to maintain enthusiasm. Negotiation will always wear us down, wear down our aspirations; we need to keep positive.

Often your counterpart will react negatively in the negotiation. Expect it, don't be threatened or worn down by it. It is simply part of his attempt to lower your aspirations. Keep positive.

Way 86 Don't be afraid to break off negotiation

Don't be afraid to break off negotiation for any reason that you believe is legitimate. If you believe that the discussion is heading in a damaging direction, or if the unexpected arises and catches you by surprise — take a break. If you are leading a team ask for time to confer privately. If you are on your own, take a short break or agree another meeting. Ask questions before you leave to ensure that you have covered and understood all the ground.

You should never be put under pressure to sign in haste. If you are being subjected to that then break for your own reasons. You might say, 'There are one or two points I need to go away and consider more carefully, perhaps we can arrange to meet again next week', or ' I would like a fresh air break; please excuse me for 30 minutes'.

Never be put under pressure to sign during or after hospitality — particularly long lunches. Use those experiences legitimately to cement relationships not to manipulate the deal. When travelling long distances particularly by air leave time before the negotiation. With transatlantic deals never agree them on the day of travel. Dehydration and jet-lag have real impact on your mind and body. You are almost certain to agree a poor deal if you settle it on the day of travel.

Way 87 Don't attack your counterpart — attack the problem

Do separate the people from the negotiation. We need to support people, and attack the problem. Understand, use phrases like, 'We really want the business to go through', then attack the problem.

There is a five-step process that can help us if we encounter some sticky personal problem or confrontation during the negotiation dialogue:

1. *Listen* to deflate. Often when confrontation arises the other person's emotions intensify. If we react to them we will allow the hot air of emotion to inflate the issue beyond its real size and importance.

2. *Sympathise* or empathise, and confirm the details. You might say 'I think I understand, if I were in your shoes I would probably feel the same. From what you are saying, the problem could be summarised like this . . . Did I get that right?' Now the tension is defused, and we are ready once again to move forward. We have identified ourselves with their feelings and made it clear that it is quite all right to feel that way.

3. *Formulate* and offer a proposed solution. Or respond with an approach of a specific trading suggestion, 'If you . . . then we . . . '.

4. *Action* any agreement made — be responsible for it.

5. *Confirm* any details verbally then be seen to write them down.

Avoid reacting to confrontation or sensitive moments. That way you will avoid attacking individuals. Where you can, try to avoid jumping to self-defence. When in that position, never use inflammatory phrases like, 'You let me down'. Instead use phrases like, 'I feel let down'. The five-step process will produce facts rather than feelings and co-opera-tion rather than confrontation.

Your counterpart will almost certainly dislike the tension of these moments. They can be quite unnerving. Try to produce an environment in which you support each other and you jointly attack any real or perceived problem.

Way 88 Don't show triumph

Don't show triumph. It creates resentment. It implies I won and he lost. Be careful who you talk to and what you say. The more you say, the more danger there is.

Any expression of elation will be interpreted negatively by your counterpart. He may begin to rue the deal and look for a way out. Be careful what you say to him, his staff or your staff. Pride goes before a fall and that is eminently applicable here. The maxim to follow is, 'Sign up then shut up'.

Way 89 Don't deal in round numbers

Round numbers cry out for attention; they shout out,'I am designed to negotiate'. Typical round numbers would be £5, £10, £100, £1000, £10,000, £100,000. There is a built in incredibility. It will weaken your position from the beginning because your counterpart will automatically expect you to concede on price. It is saying as clearly as if you put it into words, 'I don't expect to get the figure mentioned here!'

Way 90 Don't indicate movement before you need to

Don't signal willingness to move unless you want to. 'About', near', 'roughly' are words to avoid. They are words which spell movement or concession. They reveal that you are already willing to move. The phrase 'or near offer' is deadly. It is not a successful tactic for moving a deal forward; it is a concession, for nothing in return and should never be used.

In fact these words have actually become your first concession and they are offering price as the legitimate first target for your counterpart. By your own action you have removed the defensive shield from your price.

Way 91 Don't dig your heels in

Remember to focus on the overall interest. Don't take an intransigent position. Don't allow one element or one feature or one particular position to obscure the overall interest. Keep talking about that general interest. Keep the whole deal in mind, get his entire shopping list. Use a phrase like, 'What other points did you want to discuss?', or 'What are the other issues that are important to you?'

If you dig your heels in on one particular issue, the chances are that push will become shove and you will end up with breakdown or deadlock. Sometimes the intransigent position is a reflection of greed. That smells as rotten as any bad fish, and your counterpart will rightly turn up his nose at it!

Way 92 Don't be afraid to go back and try again

I shall never forget it. I was unintentionally eavesdropping in the club lounge at Heathrow and could not believe my luck! Next to me on the phone was a professional negotiator doing his stuff. Why would I be excited? Because you very rarely get to hear other professionals. This one was special. He negotiated the sale of aircraft and he had just been told he had lost a particular deal which he thought was in the bag.

For 20 minutes or so I listened to this consummate professional asking W questions. He found out how many aircraft they were finally going to buy and how much they had agreed to pay. He discovered who they had agreed it with, what the spares and maintenance agreement was. He uncovered all the terms and conditions. He discovered what negotiable variables his competitor had used, and even though he had been given a firm thumbs-down he didn't give up. While I was still sitting there he had agreed a renegotiation meeting.

When about to give up, ask yourself, 'What is wrong with one last try?'

Way 93 Don't be afraid of risk

Negotiation is risky, the only thing that is more risky is not to negotiate. You may well get it wrong, wholly or in part.

When you are negotiating be more willing to take risks and be seen to be willing, it implies confidence and will often pay off. Your counterpart will intuitively sense confidence in your approach and it will add to your authority.

Be quick to point out to your counterpart some of the risks he may be taking if he deals with another company. If you are the buyer point out to your supplier some of the riskier elements of other potential buyers, stressing the risk free environment which you may well be offering. Your financial security, your commitment to expansion, your supplier payment record terms etc.

If you are the seller, point out the security or guarantee of the USPs you offer. Show him that the absence of these attributes from other suppliers renders him vulnerable to risk. Try to quantify that risk with facts, figures, amounts and savings. Use a guarantee to eliminate the fear of risk. Deal effectively with risks your counterpart perceives, even if those risks don't really exist.

Way 94 Don't succumb to dangerous phrases

Our counterpart may well have a stockpile of dangerous phrases, which include the following:

'You scratch my back and I'll scratch yours'. Loosely interpreted, it means, 'If you give something away to me, I will give you something less valuable in return'.

'Just two or three minor things to clear up'. The interpretation would be, 'I am just about to ask you for something outrageous'.

'What I am about to suggest will be to your advantage', meaning, 'My next concession is practically worthless to you'.

'I think we are almost there'. Which being translated means, 'I think I've got you and I would like to sign up rather quickly please'.

These phrases and others like them tend to appear just before agreement, and can easily throw us off course. Beware of them and be ready for them. A simple catch-all reply can be, 'I'm not sure about that, but if you . . . then we . . . '.

Way 95 Don't be afraid to make your counterpart work hard

The harder he works the greater his satisfaction. How he got the deal he got is important. In this context, when about to say 'Yes', ask yourself what else you could achieve before agreeing. Don't rush into concluding even if it is near. Develop a habit of waiting just before agreement is expressed and ask for a little more.

When you have finished you might say, 'You are a difficult person to persuade'. It verbalises respect and appreciation.

Three Specific Techniques

Way 96 Specific tips for negotiating print and promotion

Just about everyone in business, owner manager, buyer and seller gets involved in negotiating print and promotion. These tips may well help to reduce your costs and improve your end results.

When looking at negotiable variables or concessions ask; what if:

- I prepare all the copy for the publication on your behalf

- I supply all the text on disk

- I collect the finished product (instead of a delivery charge)

- I provide all photography

- I buy the paper separately and supply to the printer

- I provide all the page planning and structure of the publication

- I could place this level of business regularly

- I can introduce you personally to four other individuals who all place print at this kind of volume.

Or you might say, 'I am an office supply company and would like to discuss supplying some office equipment in exchange for ...'.

Way 97 Price rises — how to get it wrong

I was in my mid-twenties and had secured my biggest ever negotiated deal to date, with a major international computer supplier. The deal was worth £3–4 million over a number of years. I was delighted with the deal, with the presentation we had made. I was particularly delighted with the warm relationships we had developed with the buying team. I was especially pleased to have developed what I thought was a warm strategic relationship with the Head of Buying, Europe.

The work went well until, one fateful day following a price hike from our suppliers, we wrote to inform our customer that there was going to be an unavoidable price rise in force, one month from now. By return I got the strongest letter imaginable from my favoured Head of Buying, Europe. In it he put an immediate stop to all new business. He made it clear there was no way that they would tolerate this price rise. He equally made it clear that he felt he had been dealt with in a very shoddy manner.

He demanded to see me personally and quickly. He was a shrewd and wise negotiator. When I went to see him he was his kindly self and we did agree a price rise eventually, although you don't need me to tell you that my aspirations were more than a little dented, and I did not achieve my target figure.

Way 98 Do research before you buy

If you know what you want to buy and you know who you want to buy from, then gather information first. Go with press cuttings, ring around to assess a broad range of prices. Go with printed special offers go with price lists and say, 'I really want to buy from you — this is the price offered elsewhere'.

Gill Greenwood was buying two office desks recently. She shopped around and secured some competitive quotes. She rang up her preferred supplier and asked for a quotation. She was given a price of £375. She told the salesman that she had quotes for £275, what could he do? He came back some hours later and said I can offer you a price of £275. Gill said,

I can give you the order for another £10 reduction on each'. She got the deal. Doesn't that show how just a few minutes on the phone can save you in this case £110 × 2. Just say you did that four times per month, ten months in the year. You have just added £8,800 to your profit.

Final Words

Way 99 The ones that nearly got away

Here are some powerful one-liners. Not comprehensive enough to make a Way of their own but add them up and be impressed!

Don't exaggerate facts. Don't 'elasticate' the hard information. Honesty and integrity always pay off in the end. Act dishonestly and you launch a boomerang. It has the uncanny ability of coming back and hitting you on the head!

Don't assume facts. Don't assume you have judged his mood or his feelings correctly — always check with W questions.

Be patient. Delay is always frustrating, but it is always better than a bad decision. Rushed decisions are usually bad for both parties.

If you are going to introduce extra terms or extra costs, have printed proof.

Don't believe everything you are allowed to hear. Check out the validity of any key information you are allowed to overhear.

Way 100 The ten commandments

1. *Always ask for more.* It is a legitimate tactic to use 'The Shocker' with the opening offer. Remember to have clear reasons for the opening price. Those reasons must have credibility, they must appear to be legitimate.

2. *Never say yes first time* and never accept the first counter-offer.

3. *Don't succumb to price rot* — remember, it's a buyer's job to challenge high prices. It's the seller's job to ask for high prices. Don't forget the whole free market economy is geared to have a downward pressurising impact on price. For buyer and seller the rule is the same — don't succumb.

4. *Don't give away at the start that your position is negotiable.* If you use the phrase, 'It is negotiable' — you have written the buyer a blank cheque. It means you have already given away money. We should never do it.

5. *If concession is necessary, trade reluctantly*, and slowly.

6. *Don't ever change price without changing proposal.* When bargaining use the magic phrase 'If you . . . then we. . .'. Ensure you have a list of all your negotiable variables. Have at hand what can be changed and what its cost is to you.

7. *Watch bargaining activity just before a deadline.* If you imposed the deadline yourself, get higher authority to change it, if it becomes damaging to your negotiation. Always try to find your counterpart's deadlines or pressure points. Ask him what time constraints he is under. And use that information to build your authority.

8. *Avoid careless or unnecessary tough phrases.* It may well produce intransigence in your counterpart.

9. *Stop seeing price as the primary issue.* One of my friends is senior manager in a leading international forklift truck company. On one occasion he was responsible for a launch event. He negotiated a significantly lower price from one supplier — particularly compared to the other competitors. In doing so he forced the supplier to cut corners which seriously jeopardised the success of the event. It incurred other costs which he had to recover. He said to me that the key lesson for him was learning to recognise when you are forcing a supplier to compromise quality, simply to appease a price requirement. In his words, 'It is not always defeat to yield on price. In fact the reverse can be true!' It is important to remember that all the variables in and around the deal can be used to improve it. The

danger for buyers is to try intuitively to give the seller tunnel vision which sees the price and little else. Avoid it. Keep looking at all the ingredients of the deal and keep the focus off price.

10. *Keep a sense of humour.* I was bargaining furiously for a small musical instrument in Uganda. The lady was shrewd and she just would not shift below 1500 shillings. For fun I had set myself an upper limit of just 1400. I said to her, 'Where I come from my tribe would ridicule my manhood if I spent more than 1400'. She and I both laughed. We had developed a great rapport and I knew I could communicate like that without offence and without being patronising. I got the instrument and one of my colleagues with a tender conscience then gave the extra 100 shillings! If you carry on too long and too intensely the thing sours and one party will leave feeling it has been a negative experience. Ultimately we are looking for agreement. Lighten the atmosphere, so that it does not become heavy. If you can't express normal humour in the process you will not be as effective as you can be.

Way 101 How to eat the elephant

I hope this book has been an interesting and impacting read. But please don't put it down here. I promised you at the beginning that this book could easily add thousands and, for many of you, tens of thousands of pounds to your net profit.

But of course it never will. It is destined to fail, destined to be a disappointment. Why? Because you won't apply it, will you? Come on now, be honest, you are about to put this book away aren't you?

You told yourself that you would try to apply some of these principles when you next get a chance. Don't kid yourself. Do something now and there is a chance that you will make some real money. Leave it and you never will.

Write down the five key Ways that you know intuitively will give you the greatest advantage immediately.

Jot them down *now* in the space below

1 _____

2 _____

3 _____

4 _____

5 _____

Please use these at the next possible opportunity. Promise me this. If they work for you write down the next five and try them. Keep doing it and you will not only read but begin to implement *101 Ways to Negotiate More Effectively*.

Why did I call it 'How to eat the elephant'? Simply this — the only way to eat an elephant is to do it one bite at a time. In other words any daunting or sizeable task is best done in bite-size chunks. This is sometimes called the 5 per cent rule. Try to implement 100 per cent at one go and you will get demotivated quickly. However, we know from experience that if you take 5 per cent of the material at a time, it is manageable. You are likely to make it work, and you are most likely to make money! Five ways is roughly 5 per cent.

Go on, do it now. Do it for yourself, for your company, for your family.

God bless you as you put these principles into practice.

Further Reading from Kogan Page

101 Great Mission Statements
101 Ways to Better Business Writing
101 Ways to Clean Up Your Act
101 Ways to Generate Great Ideas
101 Ways to Get Great Publicity
101 Ways to Increase Your Sales
101 Ways to Make a Professional Impact
101 Ways to Make More Profits
101 Ways to Promote Your Business
101 Ways to Succeed as an Independent Consultant
and on negotiation . . .
Negotiating Skills for Business, Elizabeth M Christopher, 1996
Never Take No for an Answer, Samfrits Le Poole, 1991
Successful Negotiation, Robert B Maddux, 1989

About the author

David Oliver runs Insight Marketing. He and his team have been leading figures in training for many years and are regarded as highly experienced trainers in the specialised fields of negotiation, sales and marketing. For 15 years they have conducted training events and seminars. The seminars have gained an unrivalled reputation with places in heavy demand.

David has worked with thousands of companies and over 25,000 delegates have attended his courses. He is regularly in demand as a presenter because of his *high energy charismatic approach*.

In addition to this experience, Insight's services include specific negotiation, consultancy, in-house training and marketing audits — all of which are undertaken for clients on an individual basis.

For further information contact Insight Marketing on 01256 895529, fax 01256 895882. E.Mail dave@insmark.demon.co.uk

Snail mail is: Insight Marketing, Cricket Corner, Lynch Hill Park, Whitchurch, Hants RG28 7NF.

Index

NEGOTIATION WORKSHOPS TAILORED TO YOUR COMPANY OR YOUR DEPARTMENT

David Oliver provides negotiation workshops tailored precisely to your market and your specific application or requirements.

Aimed at your sales people, managers or buyers, these workshops should enable you to see an increase of 10 per cent in your annual net profit.

- discover how to improve your profits
- learn new ways to protect your prices
- learn how to get the best possible deal every time
- learn how to increase your confidence in six critical areas
- learn how to identify tactics used against you
- learn how to prepare countermeasures that work for you
- learn how to avoid giving too much away
- learn how and when to move in your negotiations

Telephone 01256 895529 now for details without any obligation and ask for your FREE copy of *The Negotiation Projector*.
E-mail: Dave @insmark.Demon.Co.uk